CAMBRIDGE LIBRARY COLLECTION

Books of enduring scholarly value

English Men of Letters

In the 1870s, Macmillan publishers began to issue a series of books called 'English Men of Letters' – biographies of English writers by other English writers. The general editor of the series was the journalist, critic, politician, and supporter (and later biographer) of Gladstone, John Morley (1838–1923). The aim was to provide a short introduction to each subject and his works, but also that the life should illuminate the works, and vice versa. The subjects range chronologically from Chaucer to Thackeray and Dickens, and an important feature of the series is that many of the authors (Henry James on Hawthorne, Ward on Dickens) were discussing writers of the previous generation, and some (Trollope on Thackeray) had even known their subjects personally. The series exemplifies the British approach to literary biography and criticism at the end of the nineteenth century, and also reveals which authors were at that time regarded as canonical.

Addison

W. J. Courthope's biography of politician and writer Joseph Addison (1672–1719) was published in 1884 in the first series of English Men of Letters. Educated at Harrow and Oxford, Courthope (1842–1917) was elected fellow of the British Academy in 1907. His scholarly works include a biography and edition of the works of Alexander Pope. This work begins not with an account of Addison's birth and childhood but instead with an essay on 'The State of English Society and Letters after the Restoration', contextualising a writer whose periodical essays were still widely read and enjoyed in the late nineteenth century. The book focuses more on Addison's literary career than his political activity in support of the Whigs, devoting chapters to his work for *The Tatler*, *The Spectator* (which he co-founded with Richard Steele) and *The Guardian*, his tragedy *Cato*, and his notorious quarrel with Pope.

Cambridge University Press has long been a pioneer in the reissuing of out-of-print titles from its own backlist, producing digital reprints of books that are still sought after by scholars and students but could not be reprinted economically using traditional technology. The Cambridge Library Collection extends this activity to a wider range of books which are still of importance to researchers and professionals, either for the source material they contain, or as landmarks in the history of their academic discipline.

Drawing from the world-renowned collections in the Cambridge University Library, and guided by the advice of experts in each subject area, Cambridge University Press is using state-of-the-art scanning machines in its own Printing House to capture the content of each book selected for inclusion. The files are processed to give a consistently clear, crisp image, and the books finished to the high quality standard for which the Press is recognised around the world. The latest print-on-demand technology ensures that the books will remain available indefinitely, and that orders for single or multiple copies can quickly be supplied.

The Cambridge Library Collection will bring back to life books of enduring scholarly value (including out-of-copyright works originally issued by other publishers) across a wide range of disciplines in the humanities and social sciences and in science and technology.

Addison

WILLIAM COURTHOPE

CAMBRIDGE
UNIVERSITY PRESS

CAMBRIDGE UNIVERSITY PRESS

Cambridge, New York, Melbourne, Madrid, Cape Town,
Singapore, São Paolo, Delhi, Tokyo, Mexico City

Published in the United States of America by Cambridge University Press, New York

www.cambridge.org
Information on this title: www.cambridge.org/9781108034425

© in this compilation Cambridge University Press 2011

This edition first published 1884
This digitally printed version 2011

ISBN 978-1-108-03442-5 Paperback

English Men of Letters

EDITED BY JOHN MORLEY

ADDISON

ADDISON

BY

W. J. COURTHOPE

London:

MACMILLAN AND CO.

1884

The Right of Translation and Reproduction is Reserved.

CONTENTS.

CONTENTS.

ADDISON.

CHAPTER I.

THE STATE OF ENGLISH SOCIETY AND LETTERS
AFTER THE RESTORATION.

OF the four English men of letters whose writings most
fully embody the spirit of the eighteenth century the one
who provides the biographer with the scantiest materials
is Addison. In his *Journal to Stella*, his social verses,
and his letters to his friends, we have a vivid picture of
those relations with women and that protracted suffering
which invest with such tragic interest the history of
Swift. Pope, by the publication of his own correspondence, has enabled us, in a way that he never intended,
to understand the strange moral twist which distorted a
nature by no means devoid of noble instincts. Johnson
was fortunate in the companionship of perhaps the best
biographer who ever lived. But of the real life and
character of Addison scarcely any contemporary record
remains. The formal narrative prefixed to his works by
Tickell is, by that writer's own admission, little more than
a bibliography. Steele, who might have told us more
than any man about his boyhood and his manner of life
in London, had become estranged from his old friend

Œ   B

before his death.   No writer has taken the trouble to
preserve any account of the wit and wisdom that
enlivened the "little senate" at Button's.   His own
letters are, as a rule, compositions as finished as his papers
in the *Spectator*.   Those features in his character which
excite the greatest interest have been delineated by the
hand of an enemy—an enemy who possessed an unrivalled
power of satirical portrait-painting, and was restrained
by no regard for truth from creating in the public mind
such impressions about others as might serve to heighten
the favourable opinion of himself.

This absence of dramatic incident in Addison's life
would lead us naturally to conclude that he was deficient
in the energy and passion which cause a powerful nature
to leave a mark upon its age.   Yet such a judgment
would certainly be erroneous.   Shy and reserved as he
was, the unanimous verdict of his most illustrious contemporaries is decisive as to the respect and admiration
which he excited among them.   The man who could
exert so potent an influence over the mercurial Steele ;
who could fascinate the haughty and cynical intellect of
Swift ; whose conversation, by the admission of his
satirist Pope, had in it something more charming than
that of any other man ; of whom it was said that he
might have been chosen king if he wished it ; such a
man, though to the coarse perception of Mandeville he
might have seemed no more than "a parson in a tye-
wig," can hardly have been deficient in force of character.

Nor would it have been possible for a writer distinguished by mere elegance and refinement to leave a
lasting impress on the literature and society of his
country.   In one generation after another men, repre-

senting opposing elements of rank, class, interest, and taste, have agreed in acknowledging Addison's extraordinary merits. " Whoever wishes," says Johnson— at the end of a biography strongly coloured with the prepossessions of a semi-Jacobite Tory—" whoever wishes to attain an English style, familiar but not coarse, and elegant but not ostentatious, must give his days and nights to the volumes of Addison." " Such a mark of national respect," says Macaulay, the best representative of middle-class opinion in the present century, speaking of the statue erected to Addison in Westminster Abbey, " was due to the unsullied statesman, to the accomplished scholar, to the master of pure English eloquence, to the consummate painter of life and manners. It was due, above all, to the great satirist who alone knew how to use ridicule without abusing it; who, without inflicting a wound, effected a great social reform, and who reconciled wit and virtue, after a long and disastrous separation, during which wit had been led astray by profligacy and virtue by fanaticism."

This verdict of a great critic is accepted by an age to which the grounds of it are perhaps not very apparent. The author of any ideal creation—a poem, a drama, or a novel—has an imprescriptible property in the fame of his work. But to harmonise conflicting social elements, to bring order out of chaos in the sphere of criticism, to form right ways of thinking about questions of morals, taste, and breeding, are operations of which the credit, though it is certainly to be ascribed to particular individuals, is generally absorbed by society itself. Macaulay's eulogy is as just as it is eloquent, but the pages of the *Spectator* alone will hardly show the reader

why Addison should be so highly praised for having
reconciled wit with virtue.   Nor, looking at him as a
critic, will it appear a great achievement to have pointed
out to English society the beauties of *Paradise Lost*,
unless it be remembered that the taste of the preceding
generation still influenced Addison's contemporaries, and
that in that generation Cowley was accounted a greater
poet than Milton.

    To estimate Addison at his real value we must regard
him as the chief architect of Public Opinion in the
eighteenth century.   But here again we are met by an
initial difficulty, because it has become almost a com-
monplace of contemporary criticism to represent the
eighteenth century as a period of sheer destruction.   It
is tacitly assumed by a school of distinguished philosophical writers that we have arrived at a stage in the
world's history in which it is possible to take a positive
and scientific view of human affairs.   As it is of course
necessary that from such a system all belief in the super-
natural shall be jealously excluded, it has not seemed
impossible to write the history of Thought itself in the
eighteenth century.   And in tracing the course of this
supposed continuous stream it is natural that all the great
English writers of the period should be described as in
one way or another helping to pull down, or vainly to
strengthen, the theological barriers erected by centuries
of bigotry against the irresistible tide of enlightened
progress.

    It would be of course entirely out of place to discuss
here the merits of this new school of history.   Those
who consider that, whatever glimpses we may obtain of
the law and order of the universe, man is, as he always

has been and always will be, a mystery to himself, will hardly allow that the operations of the human spirit can be traced in the dissecting-room. But it is, in any case, obvious that to treat the great *imaginative* writers of any age as if they were only mechanical agents in an evolution of thought is to do them grave injustice. Such writers are above all things creative. Their first aim is to " show the very age and body of the time his form and pressure." No work of the eighteenth century, composed in a consciously destructive spirit, has taken its place among the acknowledged classics of the language. Even the *Tale of a Tub* is to be regarded as a satire upon the aberrations of theologians from right reason, not upon the principles of Christianity itself. The *Essay on Man* has, no doubt, logically a tendency towards Deism, but nobody ever read the poem for the sake of its philosophy ; and it is well known that Pope was much alarmed when it was pointed out to him that his conclusions might be represented as incompatible with the doctrines of revealed religion.

The truth indeed seems to be the exact converse of what is alleged by the scientific historians. So far from the eighteenth century in England being an age of destructive analysis, its energies were chiefly devoted to political, social, and literary reconstruction. Whatever revolution in faith and manners the English nation had undergone had been the work of the two preceding centuries, and, though the historic foundations of society remained untouched, the whole form of the superstructure had been profoundly modified.

"So tenacious are we," said Burke towards the close of the last century, " of our old ecclesiastical modes and fashions

of institution that very little change has been made in them
since the fourteenth or fifteenth centuries, adhering in this
particular as in all else to our old settled maxim never
entirely nor at once to depart from antiquity.   We found
these institutions on the whole favourable to morality and
discipline, and we thought they were susceptible of amendment without altering the ground.   We thought they were
capable of receiving and meliorating and, above all, of preserving the accessories of science and literature as the order
of Providence should successively produce them.   And after
all, with this Gothic and monkish education (for such it is
the groundwork), we may put in our claim to as ample and
early a share in all the improvements in science, in arts,
and in literature which have illuminated the modern world
as any other nation in Europe.   We think one main cause
of this improvement was our not despising the patrimony of
knowledge which was left us by our forefathers."

All this is, in substance, true of our political as well as
our ecclesiastical institutions.   And yet, when Burke
wrote, the great feudal and mediæval structure of England
had been so transformed by the Wars of the Roses, the
Reformation, the Rebellion, and the Revolution, that its
ancient outlines were barely visible.   In so far, therefore,
as his words seem to imply that the social evolution he
describes was produced by an imperceptible and almost
mechanical process of national instinct, the impression
they tend to create is entirely erroneous.

If we have been hitherto saved from such corruption
as undermined the republics of Italy, from the religious
wars that so long enfeebled and divided Germany, and
from the Revolution that has severed modern France
from her ancient history, thanks for this are due partly no
doubt to favouring conditions of nature and society, but
quite as much to the genius of great individuals who prepared the mind of the nation for the gradual assimila-

tion of new ideas.   Thus Langland and Wycliffe and
their numerous followers, long before the Reformation,
had so familiarised the minds of the people with their
ideas of the Christian religion that the Sovereign was
able to assume the Headship of the Church without the
shock of a social convulsion.   Fresh feelings and instincts
grew up in the hearts of whole classes of the nation
without at first producing any change in outward
habits of life, and even without arousing a sense of their
logical incongruity.   These mixed ideas were constantly
brought before the imagination in the works of the poets.
Shakespeare abounds with passages in which, side by
side with the old feudal, monarchical, catholic, and
patriotic instincts of Englishmen, we find the sentiments
of the Italian Renaissance.   Spenser conveys Puritan
doctrines sometimes by the mouth of shepherds, whose
originals he had found in Theocritus and Virgil; sometimes under allegorical forms derived from books of
chivalry and the ceremonial of the Catholic Church.
Milton, the most rigidly Calvinistic of all the English
poets in his opinions, is also the most severely classical
in his style.

It was the task of Addison to carry on the reconciling traditions of our literature.   It is his praise to
have accomplished his task under conditions far more
difficult than any that his predecessors had experienced.
What they had done was to give instinctive and characteristic expression to the floating ideas of the society about
them ; what Addison and his contemporaries did was to
found a public opinion by a conscious effort of reason
and persuasion.   Before the Civil Wars there had been
at least no visible breach in the principle of Authority

in Church and State. At the beginning of the eighteenth
century constituted authority had been recently over-
thrown ; one king had been beheaded, another had been
expelled ; the Episcopalian form of Church Government
had been violently displaced in favour of the Presbyterian, and had been with almost equal violence restored.
Whole classes of the population had been drawn into
opposing camps during the Civil War, and still stood
confronting each other with all the harsh antagonism of
sentiment inherited from that conflict. Such a bare
summary alone is sufficient to indicate the nature of the
difficulties Addison had to encounter in his efforts to
harmonise public opinion ; but a more detailed examination of the state of society after the Restoration is
required to place in its full light the extraordinary
merits of the success that he achieved.

There was, to begin with, a vehement opposition
between town and country. In the country the old
ideas of Feudalism, modified by circumstances, but
vigorous and deep-rooted, still prevailed. True, the
military system of land-tenure had disappeared with the
Restoration, but it was not so with the relations of life
and the habits of thought and feeling which the system
had created. The features of surviving Feudalism have
been inimitably preserved for us in the character of Sir
Roger de Coverley. Living in the patriarchal fashion,
in the midst of tenants and retainers, who looked up to
him as their chief, and for whose welfare and protection
he considered himself responsible, the country gentleman
valued above all things the principle of Loyalty. To
the monied classes in the towns he was instinctively
opposed ; he regarded their interests, both social and

commercial, as contrary to his own; he looked with dislike and suspicion on the economical principles of government and conduct on which these classes naturally rely. Even the younger sons of county families had in Addison's day abandoned the custom, common enough in the feudal times, of seeking their fortune in trade. Many a Will Wimble now spent his whole life in the country, training dogs for his neighbours, fishing their streams, making whips for their young heirs, and even garters for their wives and daughters.[1]

The country gentlemen were confirmed in these ideas by the difficulties of communication. During his visit to Sir Roger de Coverley the *Spectator* observed the extreme slowness with which fashions penetrated into the country; and he noticed, too, that party spirit was much more violent there than in the towns. The learning of the clergy, many of whom resided with the country squires as chaplains, was of course enlisted on the Tory side, and supplied it with arguments which the body of the party might perhaps have found it difficult to discover, or at least to express, for themselves. For Tory tastes undoubtedly lay generally rather in the direction of sport than of books. Sir Roger seems to be as much above the average level of his class as Squire Western is certainly below it: perhaps the Tory fox-hunter of the *Freeholder*, though somewhat satirically painted, is a fair representative of the society which had its headquarters at the October Club, and whose favourite poet was Tom D'Urfey.

The commercial and professional classes, from whom the Whigs derived their chief support, of course

---

[1] *Spectator*, No. 108.

predominated in the towns, and their larger opportunities of association gave them an influence in affairs
which compensated for their inferiority in numbers.
They lacked, however, what the country party possessed,
a generous ideal of life. Though many of them were
connected with the Presbyterian system, their common
sense made them revolt from its rigidity, while at the
same time their economical principles failed to supply
them with any standard that could satisfy the imagination. Sir Andrew Freeport excites in us less interest
than any member of the Spectator's Club. There was
not yet constituted among the upper middle classes that
mixed conception of good feeling, good breeding, and
good taste which we now attach to the name of "gentleman."

Two main currents of opinion divided the country, to
one of which a man was obliged to surrender himself if he
wished to enjoy the pleasures of organised society. One
of these was Puritanism, but this was undoubtedly the
less popular, or at least the less fashionable. A protracted experience of Roundhead tyranny under the
Long Parliament had inclined the nation to believe that
almost any form of Government was preferable to that
of the Saints. The Puritan, no longer the mere sectarian,
as in the days of Elizabeth and James I., somewhat
ridiculous in the extravagance of his opinions, but
respectable from the constancy with which he maintained
them, had ruled over them as a taskmaster, and had
forced them, as far as he could by military violence, to
practise the asceticism to which monks and nuns had
voluntarily submitted themselves. The most innocent
as well as the most brutal diversions of the people were

sacrificed to his spiritual pride. As Macaulay well says, he hated bear-baiting, not because it gave pain to the bear, but because it gave pleasure to the spectator. The tendency of his creed was, in fact, anti-social. Beauty in his eyes was a snare, and pleasure a sin; the only mode of social intercourse which he approved was a sermon.

On the other hand, the habits of the Court, which gave the tone to all polite society, were almost equally distasteful to the instincts of the people. It was inevitable that the inclinations of Charles II. should be violently opposed to every sentiment of the Puritans. While he was in the power of the Scots he had been forced into feigned compliance with Presbyterian rites; the Puritans had put his father to death, and had condemned himself to many years of exile and hardship in Catholic countries. He had returned to his own land half French in his political and religious sympathies, and entirely so in his literary tastes. To convert and to corrupt those of his subjects who immediately surrounded him was an easy matter. "All by the king's example lived and loved." Poets, painters, and actors were forward to promote principles viewed with favour by their sovereign and not at all disagreeable to themselves. An ingenious philosopher elevated Absolutism into an intellectual and moral system, the consequence of which was to encourage the powerful in the indulgence of every selfish instinct. As the Puritans had oppressed the country with a system of inhuman religion and transcendental morality, so now, in order to get as far from Puritanism as possible, it seemed necessary for every one aspiring to be thought a gentleman to avow himself an atheist or a debauchee.

The ideas of the man in the mode after the Restoration are excellently hit off in one of the fictitious letters in the *Spectator :*—

"I am now between fifty and sixty, and had the honour to be well with the first men of taste and gallantry in the joyous reign of Charles the Second. As for yourself, Mr. Spectator, you seem with the utmost arrogance to undermine the very fundamentals upon which we conducted ourselves. It is monstrous to set up for a man of wit and yet deny that honour in a woman is anything but peevishness, that inclination is not the best rule of life, or virtue and vice anything else but health and disease. We had no more to do but to put a lady in a good humour, and all we could wish followed of course. Then, again, your Tully and your discourses of another life are the very bane of mirth and good humour. Pry'thee don't value thyself on thy reason at that exorbitant rate and the dignity of human nature ; take my word for it, a setting dog has as good reason as any man in England." [1]

While opinions, which from different sides struck at the very roots of society, prevailed both in the fashionable and religious portions of the community, it was inevitable that Taste should be hopelessly corrupt. All the artistic and literary forms which the Court favoured were of the romantic order, but it was romance from which beauty and vitality had utterly disappeared. Of the two great principles of ancient chivalry, Love and Honour, the last notes of which are heard in the lyrics of Lovelace and Montrose, one was now held to be non-existent, and the other was utterly perverted. The feudal spirit had surrounded woman with an atmosphere of mystical devotion, but in the reign of Charles II. the passion of love was subjected to the torturing treatment then known as "wit." Cowley and Waller seem to

[1] *Spectator*, No. 158.

think that when a man is in love the energy of his feelings is best shown by discovering resemblances between his mistress and those objects in nature to which she is apparently most unlike.

The ideal of Woman, as she is represented in the *Spectator*, adding grace, charity, and refinement to domestic life, had still to be created. The king himself, the presumed mirror of good taste, was notoriously under the control of his numerous mistresses ; and the highest notion of love which he could conceive was gallantry. French romances were therefore generally in vogue. All the casuistry of love which had been elaborated by Mademoiselle de Scudery was reproduced with improvements by Mrs. Aphra Behn. At the same time, as usually happens in diseased societies, there was a general longing to cultivate the simplicity of the Golden Age, and the consequence was that no person, even in the lower grades of society, who pretended to any reading, ever thought of making love in his own person. The proper tone of feeling was not acquired till he had invested himself with the pastoral attributes of Damon and Celadon, and had addressed his future wife as Amarantha or Phyllis.

The tragedies of the period illustrate this general inclination to spurious romance. If ever there was a time when the ideal of monarchy was degraded and the instincts of chivalrous action discouraged, it was in the reign of Charles II. Absorbed as he was in the pursuit of pleasure, the king scarcely attempted to conceal his weariness when obliged to attend to affairs of State. He allowed the Dutch fleet to approach his capital and to burn his own ships of war on the Thames ; he sold

Dunkirk to the French; hardly any action in his life evinces any sense of patriotism or honour. And yet we have only to glance at Johnson's *Life of Dryden* to see how all the tragedies of the time turn on the great characters, the great actions, the great sufferings of princes. The Elizabethan drama had exhibited man in every degree of life and with every variety of character; the playwright of the Restoration seldom descended below such themes as the conquest of Mexico or Granada, the fortunes of the Great Mogul, and the fate of Hannibal. This monotony of subject was doubtless in part the result of policy, for, in pitying the fortunes of Montezuma, the imagination of the spectator insensibly recalled those of Charles the Second.

Everything in these tragedies is unreal, strained, and affected. In order to remove them as far as possible from the language of ordinary life they are written in rhyme, while the astonishment of the audience is raised with big swelling words, which vainly seek to hide the absence of genuine feeling. The heroes tear their passion to tatters because they think it heroic to do so; their flights into the sublime generally drop into the ridiculous; instead of holding up the mirror to nature, their object is to depart as far as possible from common sense. Nothing exhibits more characteristically the utterly artificial feeling, both of the dramatists and the spectators, than the habit which then prevailed of dismissing the audience after a tragic play with a witty epilogue. On one occasion, Nell Gwynne, in the character of St. Catherine, was, at the end of the play, left for dead upon the stage. Her body having to be removed, the actress suddenly started to her feet, exclaiming,

"Hold! are you mad? you damned confounded dog,
I am to rise and speak the epilogue!"[1]

By way of compensation, however, the writers of the period poured forth their real feelings without reserve in their comedies. So great, indeed, is the gulf that separates our own manners from theirs, that some critics have endeavoured to defend the comic dramatists of the Restoration against the moralists on the ground that their representations of Nature are entirely devoid of reality. Charles Lamb, who loved all curiosities, and the Caroline comedians among the number, says of them :—

"They are a world of themselves almost as much as fairy-land. Take one of their characters, male or female (with few exceptions they are alike), and place it in a modern play, and my virtuous indignation shall rise against the profligate wretch as warmly as the Catos of the pit could desire, because in a modern play I am to judge of the right and the wrong. The standard of *police* is the measure of *political justice.* The atmosphere will blight it; it cannot live here. It has got into a moral world, where it has no business, from which it must needs fall headlong; as dizzy and incapable of making a stand as a Swedenborgian bad spirit that has wandered un-awares into his sphere of Good Men or Angels. But in its own world do we feel the creature is so very bad? The Fainalls and Mirabels, the Dorimants and Lady Touchwoods, in their own sphere do not offend my moral sense; in fact, they do not appeal to it at all. They seem engaged in their proper element. They break through no laws or conscientious restraints. They know of none. They have got out of Christendom into the land of—what shall I call it?—of cuckoldry—the Utopia of gallantry, where pleasure is duty and the manners perfect freedom. It is altogether a speculative scene of things, which has no reference whatever to the world that is."

---

[1] *Spectator* No. 341.

This is a very happy description of the manner in which the plays of Etherege, Shadwell, Wycherley, and Congreve affect us to-day; and it is no doubt superfluous to expend much moral indignation on works which have long since lost their power to charm; comedies in which the reader finds neither the horseplay of Aristophanes, nor the nature of Terence, nor the poetry of Shakespeare; in which there is not a single character that arouses interest, or a situation that spontaneously provokes laughter; in which the complications of plot are produced by the devices of fine gentlemen for making cuckolds of citizens, and the artifices of wives to dupe their husbands; in which the profuse wit of the dialogue might excite admiration, if it were possible to feel the smallest interest in the occasion that produced it. But to argue that these plays never represented any state of existing society is a paradox which chooses to leave out of account the contemporary attack on the stage made by Jeremy Collier, the admissions of Dryden, and all those valuable glimpses into the manners of our ancestors which are afforded by the prologues of the period.

It is sufficient to quote against Lamb the witty and severe criticism of Steele in the *Spectator* upon Etherege's *Man of the Mode :*—

"It cannot be denied but that the negligence of everything which engages the attention of the sober and valuable part of mankind appears very well drawn in this piece. But it is denied that it is necessary to the character of a fine gentleman that he should in that manner trample upon all order and decency. As for the character of Dorimant, it is more of a coxcomb than that of Fopling. He says of one of his companions that a good correspondence between them is their mutual interest. Speaking of that friend, he declares

their being much together 'makes the women think the
better of his understanding, and judge more favourably of
my reputation.   It makes him pass upon some for a man of
very good sense, and me upon others for a very civil person.'
This whole celebrated piece is a perfect contradiction to good
manners, good sense, and common honesty ; and as there is
nothing in it but what is built upon the ruin of virtue and
innocence, according to the notion of virtue in this comedy,
I take the shoemaker to be in reality the fine gentleman of
the play : for it seems he is an atheist, if we may depend
upon his character as given by the orange-woman, who is
herself far from being the lowest in the play.   She says of a
fine man who is Dorimant's companion, 'there is not such
another heathen in the town except the shoemaker.'   His
pretension to be the hero of the drama appears still more in
his own description of his way of living with his lady.
'There is,' says he, 'never a man in the town lives more
like a gentleman with his wife than I do.   I never mind her
motions ; she never inquires into mine.   We speak to one
another civilly ; hate one another heartily ; and, because it
is vulgar to lie and soak together, we have each of us our
several settle-beds.'

"That of 'soaking together' is as good as if Dorimant
had spoken it himself ; and I think, since he puts human
nature in as ugly a form as the circumstances will bear and
is a staunch unbeliever, he is very much wronged in having
no part of the good fortune bestowed in the last act.   To
speak plain of this whole work, I think nothing but being
lost to a sense of innocence and virtue can make any one see
this comedy without observing more frequent occasion to
move sorrow and indignation than mirth and laughter.   At
the same time I allow it to be nature, but it is nature in its
utmost corruption and degeneracy." [1]

The truth is that the stage after the Restoration reflects only too faithfully the manners and the sentiments
of the only society which at that period could boast of
anything like organisation.   The press, which now enables

[1] *Spectator*, No. 65.

public opinion to exercise so powerful a control over the
manners of the times, had then scarcely an existence.
No standard of female honour restrained the license of
wit and debauchery. If the clergy were shocked at the
propagation of ideas so contrary to the whole spirit of
Christianity, their natural impulse to reprove them was
checked by the fear that an apparent condemnation of
the practices of the Court might end in the triumph
of their old enemies, the Puritans. All the elements of
an old and decaying form of society that tended to
atheism, cynicism, and dissolute living, exhibited themselves therefore in naked shamelessness on the stage.
The audiences in the theatres were equally devoid of
good manners and good taste : they did not hesitate to
interrupt the actors in the midst of a serious play, while
they loudly applauded their obscene allusions. So gross
was the character of comic dialogue that women could not
venture to appear at a comedy without masks, and under
these circumstances the theatre became the natural centre
for assignations. In such an atmosphere women readily
cast off all modesty and reserve ; indeed, the choicest inde-
cencies of the times are to be found in the epilogues to the
plays which were always assigned to the female actors.

It at first sight seems remarkable that a society
inveterately corrupt should have contained in itself such
powers of purification and vitality as to discard the
literary garbage of the Restoration period in favour of
the refined sobriety which characterises the writers of
Queen Anne's reign. But, in fact, the spread of the in-
fection was confined within certain well-marked limits.
The Court moved in a sphere apart, and was altogether
too light and frivolous to exert a decided moral influ-

ence on the great body of the nation. The country gentlemen, busied on their estates, came seldom to town ; the citizens, the lawyers, and the members of the other professions steadily avoided the theatre, and regarded with equal contempt the moral and literary excesses of the courtiers. Among this class, unrepresented at present in the world of letters, except perhaps by antiquarians like Selden, the foundations of sound taste were being silently laid. The readers of the nation had hitherto been almost limited to the nobility. Books were generally published by subscription, and were dependent for their success on the favour with which they were received by the courtiers. But, after the subsidence of the Civil War, the nation began to make rapid strides in wealth and refinement, and the monied classes sought for intellectual amusement in their leisure hours. Authors by degrees found that they might look for readers beyond the select circle of their aristocratic patrons ; and the bookseller, who had hitherto calculated his profits merely by the commission he might obtain on the sale of books, soon perceived that they were becoming valuable as property. The reign of Charles II. is remarkable not only for the great increase in the number of the licensed printers in London, but for the appearance of the first of the race of modern publishers, Jacob Tonson.

The portion of society whose tastes the publishers undertook to satisfy was chiefly interested in history, poetry, and criticism. It was this for which Dryden composed his *Miscellany*, this to which he addressed the admirable critical essays which precede his *Translations from the Latin Poets* and his *Versifications of Chaucer*, and this which afterwards gave the main support to the *Tatler*

and the *Spectator*. Ignorant of the writings of the great
classical authors, as well as of the usages of polite
society, these men were nevertheless robust and manly
in their ideas, and were eager to form for themselves a
correct standard of taste by reference to the best authorities.   Though they turned with repugnance from the
playhouse and from the morals of the Court, they could
not avoid being insensibly affected by the tone of grace
and elegance which prevailed in Court circles. And in this
respect, if in no other, our gratitude is due to the Caroline dramatists, who may justly claim to be the founders
of the *social* prose style in English literature.   Before
them English prose had been employed, no doubt, with
music and majesty by many writers ; but the style of these
is scarcely representative ; they had used the language for
their own elevated purposes, without, however, attempting to give it that balanced fineness and subtlety which
makes it a fitting instrument for conveying the complex
ideas of an advanced stage of society.   Dryden, Wycherley, and their followers, impelled by the taste of the
Court to study the French language, brought to English
composition a nicer standard of logic and a more choice
selection of language, while the necessity of pleasing
their audiences with brilliant dialogue made them careful
to give their sentences that well-poised structure which
Addison afterwards carried to perfection in the *Spectator*.

By this brief sketch the reader may be enabled to
judge of the distracted state of society, both in politics
and taste, in the reign of Charles II.   On the one side,
the Monarchical element in the Constitution was represented by the Court Party, flushed with the recent
restoration ; retaining the old ideas and principles of

absolutism which had prevailed under James I., without
being able to perceive their inapplicability to the existing nature of things; feeding its imagination alternately
on sentiments derived from the decayed spirit of
chivalry, and on artistic representations of fashionable
debauchery in its most open form—a party which, while
it fortunately preserved the traditions of wit, elegance,
and gaiety of style, seemed unaware that these
qualities could be put to any other use than the mitiga-
tion of an intolerable *ennui*.   On the other side, the
rising power of Democracy found its representatives in
austere Republicans opposed to all institutions in Church
and State that seemed to obstruct their own abstract
principles of government; gloomy fanatics, who, with
an intense intellectual appreciation of eternal principles
of religion and morality, sought to sacrifice to their
system the most permanent and even innocent instincts
of human nature.   Between the two extreme parties was
the unorganised body of the nation, grouped round old
customs and institutions, rapidly growing in wealth and
numbers, conscious of the rise in their midst of new
social principles, but perplexed how to reconcile these
with time-honoured methods of religious, political, and
literary thought.   To lay the foundations of sound
opinion among the people at large; to prove that reconciliation was possible between principles hitherto exhibited only in mutual antagonism; to show that under
the English Constitution monarchy, aristocracy, and
democracy might all be harmonised, that humanity was
not absolutely incompatible with religion or morality with
art, was the task of the statesmen, and still more of the
men of letters, of the early part of the eighteenth century.

CHAPTER II.

JOSEPH ADDISON was born on the 1st of May 1672. He was the eldest son of Lancelot Addison, at the time of his birth rector of Milston, near Amesbury, in Wiltshire, and afterwards Dean of Lichfield. His father was a man of character and accomplishments. Educated at Oxford, while that University was under the control of the famous Puritan Visitation, he made no secret of his contempt for principles to which he was forced to submit, or of his preferences for Monarchy and Episcopacy. His boldness was not agreeable to the University authorities, and, being forced to leave Oxford, he maintained himself for a time near Petworth, in Sussex, by acting as chaplain or tutor in families attached to the Royalist cause. After the Restoration he obtained the appointment of chaplain to the garrison of Dunkirk, and when that town was ceded to France in 1662, he was removed in a similar capacity to Tangier. Here he remained eight years, but, venturing on a visit to England, his post was bestowed upon another, and he would have been left without resources, had not one of his friends presented him with the living of Milston, valued at £120 a year. With the courage of his order he thereupon took

a wife, Jane, daughter of Dr. Nathaniel Gulston, and
sister of William Gulston, Bishop of Bristol, by whom
he had six children, three sons and three daughters, all
born at Milston.   In 1675 he was made a prebendary of
Salisbury Cathedral and Chaplain-in-Ordinary to the
King; and in 1683 he was promoted to the Deanery of
Lichfield, as a reward for his services at Tangier, and
out of consideration of losses which he had sustained by
a fire at Milston.   His literary reputation stood high,
and it is said that he would have been made a bishop, if
his old zeal for legitimacy had not prompted him to
manifest in the Convocation of 1689 his hostility to the
Revolution.   He died in 1703.

Lancelot was a writer at once voluminous and lively.
In the latter part of his life he produced several treatises
on theological subjects, the most popular of which was
called *An Introduction to the Sacrament.*   This book
passed through many editions.   The doctrine it contains
leans rather to the Low Church side.   But much the
most characteristic of his writings were his works on
Mahommedanism and Judaism, the results of his studies
during his residence in Barbary.   These show not only
considerable industry and research and powers of shrewd
observation, but that genuine literary faculty which
enables a writer to leave upon a subject of a general
nature the impression of his own character.   While
there is nothing forced or exaggerated in his historical
style, a vein of allegory runs through the narrative of
the *Revolutions of the Kingdoms of Fez and Morocco*, which
must have had a piquant flavour for the orthodox English reader of that day.   Recollections of the Protectorate
would have taken nothing of its vividness from the por-

trait of the Moorish priest who "began to grow into reputation with the people by reason of his high pretensions to piety and fervent zeal for their law, illustrated by a stubborn rigidity of conversation and outward sanctity of life." When the Zeriffe, with ambitious designs on the throne, sent his sons on a pilgrimage to Mecca, the religious buffooneries practised by the young men must have recalled to the reader circumstances more recent and personal than those which the author was apparently describing. "Much was the reverence and reputation of holiness which they thereby acquired among the superstitious people, who could hardly be kept from kissing their garments and adoring them as saints, while they failed not in their parts, but acted as much devotion as high contemplative looks, deep sighs, tragical gestures, and other passionate interjections of holiness could express. 'Allah, allah!' was their doleful note, their sustenance the people's alms." And when these impostors had inveigled the King of Fez into a religious war, the description of those who "mistrusted their own safety and began, but too late, to repent their approving of an armed hypocrisy" was not more applicable to the rulers of Barbary than to the people of England. "Puffed up with their successes, they forgot their obedience, and these saints denied the king the fifth part of their spoils . . . By which it appeared that they took up arms, not out of love for their country and zeal for their religion, but out of desire of rule." There is, indeed, nothing in these utterances which need have prevented the writer from consistently promoting the Revolution of 1688; yet his principles seem to have carried him far in the opposite direction; and it is interesting to remember that the assertor in Convocation of the doctrine of indefeasible hereditary right was the father of the author of the *Whig Examiner* and the *Freeholder.* However decidedly Joseph may have dissented from his father's political creed, we know that he entertained admiration and respect for his memory, and that death alone prevented him from completing the monument afterwards erected in Lancelot's honour in Lichfield Cathedral.

Of Addison's mother nothing of importance is recorded. His second brother, Gulston, became Governor of Fort St. George, in the East Indies; and the third, Lancelot, followed in Joseph's footsteps so far as to obtain a Fellowship at Magdalen College, Oxford. His sisters, Jane and Anna, died young; but Dorothy was twice married, and Swift records in her honour that she was "a kind of wit, and very like her brother." We may readily believe that a writer so lively as Lancelot would have had clever children, but Steele was perhaps carried away by the zeal of friendship or the love of epigram when he said in his dedication to the *Drummer:* "Mr. Dean Addison left behind him four children, each of whom, for excellent talents and singular perfections, was as much above the ordinary world as their brother Joseph was above them." But that Steele had a sincere admiration for the whole family is sufficiently shown by his using them as an example in one of his early *Tatlers:*—

"I remember among all my acquaintance but one man whom I have thought to live with his children with equanimity and a good grace. He had three sons and one daughter, whom he bred with all the care imaginable in a liberal and

ingenuous way. I have often heard him say he had the
weakness to love one much better than the other, but that
he took as much pains to correct that as any other criminal
passion that could arise in his mind. His method was to
make it the only pretension in his children to his favour to
be kind to each other, and he would tell them that he who
was the best brother he would reckon the best son. This
turned their thoughts into an emulation for the superiority
in kind and tender affection towards each other. The boys
behaved themselves very early with a manly friendship ; and
their sister, instead of the gross familiarities and impertinent
freedoms in behaviour usual in other houses, was always
treated by them with as much complaisance as any other
young lady of their acquaintance. It was an unspeakable
pleasure to visit or sit at a meal in that family. I have often
seen the old man's heart flow at his eyes with joy upon occasions which would appear indifferent to such as were strangers
to the turn of his mind ; but a very slight accident, wherein
he saw his children's good-will to one another, created in him
the god-like pleasure of loving them because they loved each
other. This great command of himself in hiding his first
impulse to partiality at last improved to a steady justice
towards them, and that which at first was but an expedient
to correct his weakness was afterwards the measure of his
virtue." [1]

This, no doubt, is the set description of a moralist,
and to an age in which the liberty of manners has
grown into something like license it may savour of
formalism and priggishness; but when we remember
that the writer was one of the most warm-hearted of
men, and that the subject of his panegyric was himself
full of vivacity and impulse, it must be admitted that
the picture which it gives us of the Addison family in
the rectory of Milston is a particularly amiable one.

Though the eighteenth century had little of that feel-

[1] *Tatler*, No. 25.

ing for natural beauty which distinguishes our own, a man of Addison's imagination could hardly fail to be impressed by the character of the scenery in which his childhood was passed.   No one who has travelled on a summer's day across Salisbury Plain, with its vast canopy of sky and its open tracts of undulating downland, relieved by no shadows except such as are thrown by the passing cloud, the grazing sheep, and the great circle of Stonehenge, will forget the delightful sense of refreshment and repose produced by the descent into the valley of the Avon.   The sounds of human life rising from the villages after the long solitude of the plain, the shade of the deep woods, the coolness of the river, like all streams rising in the chalk, clear and peaceful, are equally delicious to the sense and the imagination.   It was, doubtless, the recollection of these scenes that inspired Addison in his paraphrase of the twenty-third Psalm :—

> " The Lord my pasture shall prepare,
>   And feed me with a shepherd's care.
>
>   .   .   .   .   .
>
>   When in the sultry glebe I faint,
>   Or on the thirsty mountain pant,
>   To fertile vales and dewy meads
>   My weary wandering steps he leads,
>   Where peaceful rivers, soft and slow,
>   Amid the verdant landscape flow."

At Amesbury he was first sent to school, his master being one Nash ; and here, too, he probably met with the first recorded adventure of his life.   It is said that, having committed some fault and being fearful of the consequences, he ran away from school, and, taking up his abode in a hollow tree, maintained himself as he could, till he was discovered and brought back to his parents. He was removed from Amesbury to Salisbury, and thence to the Grammar School at Lichfield, where he is said to have been the leader in a "barring out." From Lichfield he passed to the Charter House, then under the charge of Dr. Ellis, a man of taste and scholarship. The Charter House at that period was, after Westminster, the best-known school in England, and here was laid the foundation of that sound classical taste which perfected the style of the essays in the *Spectator*.

Macaulay labours with much force and ingenuity to prove that Addison's classical acquirements were only superficial, and, in his usual epigrammatic manner, hazards the opinion that "his knowledge of Greek, though doubtless such as was, in his time, thought respectable at Oxford, was evidently less than that which many lads now carry away every year from Eton and Rugby." That Addison was not a scholar of the class of Bentley or Porson may be readily admitted. But many scattered allusions in his works prove that his acquaintance with the Greek poets of every period, if cursory, was wide and intelligent; he was sufficiently master of the language thoroughly to understand the spirit of what he read; he undertook while at Oxford a translation of Herodotus, and one of the papers in the *Spectator* is a direct imitation of a *jeu d'esprit* of Lucian's. The Eton or Rugby boy who, in these days, with a normal appetite for cricket and football, acquired an equal knowledge of Greek literature, would certainly be somewhat of a prodigy.

No doubt, however, Addison's knowledge of the Latin

poets was, as Macaulay infers, far more extensive and profound. It would have been strange had it been otherwise. The influence of the classical side of the Italian Renaissance was now at its height, and wherever those ideas became paramount Latin composition was held in at least as much esteem as poetry in the vernacular. Especially was this the case in England, where certain affinities of character and temperament made it easy for writers to adopt Roman habits of thought. Latin verse composition soon took firm root in the public schools and universities, so that clever boys of the period were tolerably familiar with most of the minor Roman poets. Pope, in the fourth book of the *Dunciad*, vehemently attacked the tradition as confining the mind to the study of words rather than of things; but he had himself had no experience of a public school, and only those who fail to appreciate the influence of Latin verse composition on the style of our own greatest orators, and of poets like Milton and Gray, will be inclined to undervalue it as an instrument of social and literary training.

Proficiency in this art may at least be said to have laid the foundation of Addison's fortunes. Leaving the Charter House in 1687, at the early age of fifteen, he was entered at Queen's College, Oxford, and remained a member of that society for two years, when a copy of his Latin verses fell into the hands of Dr. Lancaster, then Fellow and afterwards Provost of the College. Struck with their excellence, Lancaster used his influence to obtain for him a demyship at Magdalen. The subject of this fortunate set of verses was "Inauguratio Regis Gulielmi," from which fact we may reasonably infer that even in his boyhood his mind had acquired a

Whig bias.   Whatever inclination he may have had in
this direction would have been confirmed by the associations of his new college.   The fluctuations of opinion
in Magdalen had been frequent and extraordinary.
Towards the close of Elizabeth's reign it was notorious
for its Calvinism, but under the Chancellorship of Laud
it appears to have adopted, with equal ardour, the cause
of Arminianism, for it was among the colleges that
offered the stoutest opposition to the Puritan visitors in
1647-48.   The despotic tendencies of James II., however, again cooled its loyalty, and its spirited resistance
to the king's order for the election of a Roman Catholic
President had given a mortal blow to the Stuart dynasty.
Hough was now President, but in consequence of the
dispute with the king there had been no election of
demies in 1688, so that twice the usual number was
chosen in the following year, and the occasion was distinguished by the name of the "golden election."   From
Magdalen Addison proceeded to his master's degree in
1693; the College elected him probationary Fellow in
1697, and actual Fellow the year after.   He retained his
Fellowship till 1711.

Of his tastes, habits, and friendships at Oxford there
are few records.   Among his acquaintance were Boulter,
afterwards Archbishop of Dublin—whose memory is un-
enviably perpetuated in company with Ambrose Phillips
in Pope's *Epistle to Arbuthnot*,

"Does not one table Bavius still admit,
   Still to one Bishop Phillips seem a wit ?"—

and possibly the famous Sacheverell.[1]   He is said to have

[1] A note in the edition of Johnson's *Lives of the Poets*, published
in 1801, states, on the authority of a "Lady in Wiltshire," who

shown in the society of Magdalen some of the shyness that afterwards distinguished him ; he kept late hours, and read chiefly after dinner.   The walk under the well-known elms by the Cherwell is still connected with his name.   Though he probably acted as tutor in the college, the greater part of his quiet life at the University was doubtless occupied in study.   A proof of his early maturity is seen in the fact that, in his nineteenth year, a young man of birth and fortune, Mr. Rushout, who was being educated at Magdalen, was placed under his charge.

His reputation as a scholar and a man of taste soon extended itself to the world of letters in London.   In 1693, being then in his twenty-second year, he wrote his *Account of the Greatest English Poets ;* and about the same time he addressed a short copy of verses to Dryden, complimenting him on the enduring vigour of his poetical faculty as shown in his translations of Virgil and other Latin poets, some of which had recently appeared in Tonson's *Miscellany.*   The old poet appears to have been highly gratified, and to have welcomed the advances thus made to him, for he returned Addison's compliment by bestowing high and not unmerited praise on the translation of the Fourth Book of the *Georgics*, which the latter soon after undertook, and by printing, as a preface to his own translation, a discourse written by Addison on the *Georgics*, as well as arguments to most of the books of the *Æneid.*

derived her information from a Mr. Stephens, a Fellow of Magdalen and a contemporary of Addison's, that the Henry Sacheverell to whom Addison dedicated his *Account of the Greatest English Poets* was not the well-known divine, but a personal friend of Addison's, who died young, having written a *History of the Isle of Man.*

Through Dryden, no doubt, he became acquainted
with Jacob Tonson. The father of English publishing
had for some time been a well-known figure in the
literary world. He had purchased the copyright of
Paradise Lost; he had associated himself with Dryden
in publishing before the Revolution two volumes of
Miscellanies; encouraged by the success which these
obtained, he put the poet in 1693 on some translations
of Juvenal and Persius, and two new volumes of *Miscellanies;* while in 1697 he urged him to undertake a
translation of the whole of the works of Virgil. Observing how strongly the public taste set towards the great
classical writers, he was anxious to employ men of
ability in the work of turning them into English;
and it appears from existing correspondence that he
engaged Addison, while the latter was at Oxford, to
superintend a translation of Herodotus. He also suggested a translation of Ovid. Addison undertook to
procure coadjutors for the work of translating the Greek
historian. He himself actually translated the books
called *Polymnia* and *Urania,* but for some unexplained
reason the work was never published. For Ovid he
seems, on the whole, to have had less inclination. At
Tonson's instance he translated the second book of the
Metamorphoses, which was first printed in the volume
of *Miscellanies* that appeared in 1697; but he wrote to
the publisher that "Ovid had so many silly stories with
his good ones that he was more tedious to translate than
a better poet would be." His study of Ovid, however,
was of the greatest use in developing his critical faculty;
the excesses and want of judgment in that poet forced
him to reflect, and his observations on the style of his

author anticipate his excellent remarks on the difference between True and False Wit in the sixty-second number of the *Spectator*.

Whoever, indeed, compares these notes with the *Essay on the Georgics*, and with the opinions expressed in the *Account of the English Poets*, will be convinced that the foundations of his critical method were laid at this period (1697). In the *Essay on the Georgics* he seems to be timid in the presence of Virgil's superiority; his *Account of the English Poets*, besides being impregnated with the principles of taste prevalent after the Restoration, shows deficient powers of perception and appreciation. The name of Shakespeare is not mentioned in it, Dryden and Congreve alone being selected to represent the drama. Chaucer is described as "a merry bard," whose humour has become obsolete through time and change; while the rich pictorial fancy of the *Faery Queen* is thus described:

> "Old Spenser next, warmed with poetic rage,
> In ancient tales amused a barbarous age—
> An age that yet uncultivate and rude,
> Where'er the poet's fancy led pursued,
> Through pathless fields and unfrequented floods,
> To dens of dragons and enchanted woods.
> But now the mystic tale, that pleased of yore,
> Can charm an understanding age no more;
> The long-spun allegories fulsome grow,
> While the dull moral lies too plain below."

According to Pope—always a suspicious witness where Addison is concerned—he had not read Spenser when he wrote this criticism on him.[1]

Milton, as a legitimate successor of the classics, is of course appreciated, but not at all after the elaborate

---

[1] *Spence's Anecdotes*, p. 50.

D

fashion of the *Spectator;* to Dryden, the most distinguished poet of the day, deserved compliments are paid,
but their value is lessened by the exaggerated opinion
which the writer entertains of Cowley, who is described as
a "mighty genius," and is praised for the inexhaustible
riches of his imagination. Throughout the poem, in
fact, we observe a remarkable confusion of various veins
of thought; an unjust depreciation of the Gothic grandeur
of the older English poets; a just admiration for the
Greek and Roman authors; a sense of the necessity of
good sense and regularity in writings composed for an
"understanding age;" and at the same time a lingering
taste for the forced invention and far-fetched conceits
that mark the decay of the spirit of mediæval chivalry.

With the judgments expressed in this performance
it is instructive to compare such criticisms on Shakespeare as we find in No. 42 of the *Spectator;* the papers
on "Chevy Chase" (73, 74); and particularly the following passage :—

"As true wit consists in the resemblance of ideas, and
false wit in the resemblance of words, according to the fore-
going instances, there is another kind of wit, which consists
partly in the resemblance of ideas and partly in the resemblance of words, which, for distinction's sake, I shall call
mixed wit. This kind of wit is that which abounds in
Cowley more than in any author that ever wrote. Mr. Waller
has likewise a great deal of it. Mr. Dryden is very sparing
in it. Milton has a genius much above it. *Spenser is in
the same class with Milton.* The Italians even in their epic
poetry are full of it. Monsieur Boileau, who formed himself
upon the ancient poets, has everywhere rejected it with scorn.
If we look after mixed wit among the Greeks we shall find
it nowhere but in the epigrammatists. There are indeed
some strokes of it in the little poem ascribed to Musæus,
which by that, as well as many other marks, betrays itself to

be a modern composition.   If we look into the Latin writers we find none of this mixed wit in Virgil, Lucretius, or Catullus ; very little in Horace, but a great deal of it in Ovid, and scarce anything else in Martial."

The stepping-stone from the immaturity of the early criticisms in the *Account of the Greatest English Poets* to the finished ease of the *Spectator* is to be found in the notes to the translation of Ovid.[1]

The time came when he was obliged to form a decision affecting the entire course of his life.   Tonson, who had a wide acquaintance, no doubt introduced him to Congreve and the leading men of letters in London, and through them he was presented to Somers and Montague. Those ministers perhaps persuaded him, as a point of etiquette, to write in 1695, his *Address to King William*, a poem composed in a vein of orthodox hyperbole, all of which must have been completely thrown away on that most unpoetical of monarchs.   Yet in spite of those seductions Addison lingered at Oxford.   To retain his Fellowship it was necessary for him to take orders.   Had he done so, there can be no doubt that his literary skill and his value as a political partizan would have opened for him a road to the highest preferment.   At that time the clergy were far from thinking it unbecoming to their cloth to fight in the political arena or to take part in journalism.   Swift would have been advanced to a bishopric as a reward for his political services if it had not been for the prejudice entertained towards him by Queen Anne ; Boulter, rector of St. Saviour's, Southwark, having made himself conspicuous by editing a

[1] Compare the *Notes on the Metamorphoses*, Fab. v. (Tickell's edition, vol. vi. p. 183), where the substance of the above passage is found in embryo.

paper called the *Freethinker*, was raised to the Primacy
of Ireland ; Hoadley, the notorious Bishop of Bangor,
edited the *London Journal ;* the honours that were
awarded to two men of such second-rate intellectual
capacity would hardly have been denied to Addison.
He was inclined in this direction by the example and
advice of his father, who was now Dean of Lichfield,
and who was urgent on his son to rid himself of the
pecuniary embarrassments in which he was involved, by
embracing the Church as a profession.   A few years
before he had himself seemed to look upon the Church
as his future sphere.   In his *Account of the Greatest
English Poets*, he says :—

> " I leave the arts of poetry and verse
> To them that practise them with more success.
> Of greater truths I'll now propose to tell,
> And so at once, dear friend and muse, farewell."

Had he followed up his intention we might have
known the name of Addison as that of an artful contro-
versialist, and perhaps as a famous writer of sermons ;
but we should, in all probability, have never heard of the
Spectator.

Fortunately for English letters other influences prevailed to give a different direction to his fortunes.   It is
true that Tickell, Addison's earliest biographer, states
that his determination not to take orders was the result
of his own habitual self-distrust, and of a fear of the
responsibilities which the clerical office would involve.
But Steele, who was better acquainted with his friend's
private history, on reading Tickell's Memoir, addressed a
letter to Congreve on the subject, in which he says :—

> " These, you know very well, were not the reasons which

made Mr. Addison turn his thoughts to the civil world ; and, as you were the instrument of his becoming acquainted with Lord Halifax, I doubt not but you remember the warm instances that noble lord made to the head of the College not to insist upon Mr. Addison's going into orders. His arguments were founded upon the general pravity and corruption of men of business, who wanted liberal education. And I remember, as if I had read the letter yesterday, that my lord ended with a compliment, that, however he might be represented as a friend to the Church, he never would do it any other injury than keeping Mr. Addison out of it."

No doubt the real motive of the interest in Addison shown by Lord Halifax, at that time known as Charles Montague, was an anxiety which he shared with all the leading statesmen of the period, and of which more will be said presently, to secure for his party the services of the ablest writers. Finding his *protégé* as yet hardly qualified to transact affairs of State, he joined with Lord Somers, who had also fixed his eyes on Addison, in soliciting for him from the Crown in 1699 a pension of £300 a year, which might enable him to supplement his literary accomplishments with the practical experience of travel. Addison naturally embraced the offer. He looked forward to studying the political institutions of foreign countries, to seeing the spots of which he had read in his favourite classical authors, and to meeting the most famous men of letters on the Continent.

It is characteristic both of his own tastes and of his age that he seems to have thought his best passport to intellectual society abroad would be his Latin poems. His verses on the *Peace of Ryswick*, written in 1697 and dedicated to Montague, had already procured him great reputation, and had been praised by

Edmund Smith—a high authority—as "the best Latin
poem since the *Æneid*." This gave him the opportunity
of collecting his various compositions of the same kind,
and in 1699 he published from the Sheldonian Press a
second volume of the *Musæ Anglicanæ*—the first having
appeared in 1691—containing poems by various Oxford
scholars. Among the contributors were Hannes, one of
the many scholarly physicians of the period ; J. Philips,
the author of the *Splendid Shilling;* and Alsop, a prominent antagonist of Bentley, whose Horatian humour
is celebrated by Pope in the *Dunciad.*[1]

But the most interesting of the names in the volume is
that of the once celebrated Edmond, commonly called
" Rag," Smith, author of the *Ode on the Death of Dr. Pocock*,
who seems to have been among Addison's intimate
acquaintance, and deserves to be recollected in connection with him on account of a certain similarity in their
genius and the extraordinary difference in their fortunes.
" Rag " was a man of fine accomplishments and graceful
humour, but, like other scholars of the same class,
indolent and licentious. In spite of great indulgence
extended to him by the authorities of Christ Church, he
was expelled from the University in consequence of his
irregularities. His friends stood by him, and, through
the interest of Addison, a proposal was made to him to
undertake a history of the Revolution, which, however,
from political scruples he felt himself obliged to decline.
Like Addison, he wrote a tragedy modelled on classical
lines ; but, as it had no political significance, it only pleased
the critics, without, like " Cato," interesting the public.
Like Addison, too, he had an opportunity of profiting

[1] *Dunciad,* Book iv. 224.

by the patronage of Halifax, but laziness or whim
prevented him from keeping an appointment which
the latter had made with him, and caused him to miss
a place worth £300 a year. Addison, by his own
exertions, rose to posts of honour and profit, and towards
the close of his life became Secretary of State. Smith
envied his advancement, and, ignoring the fact that his
own failure was entirely due to himself, murmured at
fortune for leaving him in poverty. Yet he estimated
his wants at £600 a year, and died of indulgence when
he can scarcely have been more than forty years of age.

Addison's compositions in the *Musæ Anglicanæ* are
eight in number. All of them are distinguished by the
ease and flow of the versification, but they are generally
wanting in originality. The best of them is the *Pygmæo-
Gerano-Machia*, which is also interesting as showing traces
of that rich vein of humour which Addison worked out
in the *Tatler* and *Spectator*. The mock-heroic style in
prose and verse was sedulously cultivated in England
throughout the eighteenth century. Swift, Pope,
Arbuthnot, and Fielding, developed it in various
forms ; but Addison's Latin poem is perhaps the first
composition in which the fine fancy and invention, afterwards shown in the *Rape of the Lock* and *Gulliver's
Travels*, conspicuously displayed itself.

A literary success of this kind at that epoch gave a
writer a wider reputation than he could gain by compositions in his own language. Armed, therefore, with
copies of the *Musæ Anglicanæ* for presentation to scholars,
and with Halifax's recommendatory letters to men of
political distinction, Addison started for the Continent.

CHAPTER III.

TRAVELLING in the seventeenth and eighteenth centuries involved an amount of thought and precaution which would have seemed inconvenient to the tourist accustomed to abandon himself to the authority of guide-books, couriers, and railway companies. By ardent spirits like Roderick Random it was regarded as the sphere of enterprise and fortune, and not without reason, in days when adventures were to be met with on almost every road in the country, and in the streets and inns of the towns. The graver portion of society, on the other hand, considered it as part of the regular course of education through which every young man of position ought to pass before entering into active life. French was the universally recognised language of diplomacy. French manners and conversation were considered to be the best school for politeness, while Italy was held in the highest respect by the northern nations as the source of revived art and letters. Some of the most distinguished Englishmen of the time looked, it is true, with little favour on this fashionable training. " Lord Cowper," says Spence, on the information of Dr. Conybeare, " on his death-bed ordered that his son should never travel (it is by the

absolute desire of the Queen that he does). He ordered
this from a good deal of observation on its effects ; he
had found that there was little to be hoped, and much to
be feared, from travelling. Atwell, who is the young
lord's tutor abroad, gives but a very discouraging account
of it too in his letters; and seems to think that people
are sent out too young, and are too hasty to find any
great good from it."

On some of the stronger and more enthusiastic minds
the chief effect of the grand tour was to produce a violent
hatred of all foreign manners. Dennis, the critic, for
instance, who, after leaving Cambridge, spent some time
on the Continent, returned with a confirmed dislike to
the French, and ostentatiously displayed in his writings
how much he held "dragoons and wooden shoes in
scorn," and it is amusing to find Addison at a later date
making his Tory fox-hunter declare this anti-Gallican
temper to be the main fruits of foreign travel.

But, in general, what was intended to be a school for
manners and political instruction proved rather a source
of unsettlement and dissipation ; and the vigorous and
glowing lines in which Pope makes the tutor describe to
Dulness the doings of the "young Æneas" abroad, may
be taken as a faithful picture of the travelled pupil of the
period.

> " Intrepid then o'er seas and land he flew ;
> Europe he saw, and Europe saw him too.
> There all thy gifts and graces we display,
> Thou, only thou, directing all our way!
> To where the Seine, obsequious as she runs,
> Pours at great Bourbon's feet her silken sons ;
> Or Tyber, now no longer Roman, rolls,
> Vain of Italian arts, Italian souls :

To happy convents bosomed deep in vines,
Where slumber abbots purple as their wines :
To isles of fragrance, lily-silvered vales,
Diffusing languor in the panting gales:
To lands of singing or of dancing slaves,
Love-whispering woods, and lute-resounding waves.
But chief her shrine where naked Venus keeps,
And Cupids ride the lion of the deeps ;
Where, eased of fleets, the Adriatic main
Wafts the smooth eunuch and enamoured swain.
Led by my hand, he sauntered Europe round,
And gathered every vice on Christian ground ;
Saw every court, heard every king declare
His royal sense of operas or the fair ;
The stews and palace equally explored,
Intrigued with glory, and with spirit whored;
Tried all *hors-d'œuvres*, all liqueurs defined,
Judicious drank, and greatly daring dined ;
Dropped the dull lumber of the Latin store,
Spoiled his own language, and acquired no more ;
All classic learning lost on classic ground ;
And last turned air, the echo of a sound."

It is needless to say that Addison's experiences of
travel were of a very different kind. He left England
in his twenty-eighth year, with a mind well equipped
from a study of the best authors, and with the intention
of qualifying himself for political employment at home,
after familiarising himself with the languages and
manners of foreign countries. His sojourn abroad
extended over four years, and his experience was more
than usually varied and comprehensive. Crossing from
Dover to Calais some time in the summer of 1699, he
spent nearly eighteen months in France making himself
master of the language. In December 1700 he embarked
at Marseilles for a tour in Italy, and visited in succession
the following places :—Monaco, Genoa, Pavia, Milan,

Brescia, Verona, Padua, Venice, Ferrara, Ravenna, Rimini,
S. Marino, Pesaro, Fano, Sinigaglia, Ancona, Loreto,
Rome (where, as it was his intention to return, he only
visited St. Peter's and the Pantheon), Naples, Capri,
whence he came back to Rome by sea, the various towns
in the neighbourhood of Rome, Siena, Leghorn, Pisa,
Lucca, Florence, Bologna, Modena, Parma, and Turin.
Thus, in the course of this journey, which lasted exactly
a twelvemonth, he twice crossed the Apennines, and
made acquaintance with all the more important cities in
the northern part of the Peninsula.   In December 1701
he passed over Mont Cenis to Geneva, proceeding then
by Fribourg, Berne, Soleure, Zurich, St. Gall, Linden,
Insbruck, Hall, to Vienna, where he arrived in the
autumn of 1702.   After making a brief stay in the
Austrian capital he turned his face homewards, and having visited the Protestant cities of Germany, and made a
rather longer stay in Hamburg than in any other, he
reached Holland in the spring of 1703, and remained in
that country till his return to England some time in the
autumn of the same year.

During his journey he made notes for his *Remarks on
Italy*, which he published immediately on his return home,
and he amused himself while crossing Mont Cenis, with
composing his *Letter to Lord Halifax*, which contains,
perhaps, the best verses he ever wrote.   Though the
ground over which he passed was well trodden, and though
he possessed none of the special knowledge which gives
value to the observations of travellers like Arthur Young,
yet his remarks on the people and places he saw are the
product of an original mind, and his illustrations of his
route from the Latin poets are remarkably happy and

graceful.   It is interesting also to observe how many of
the thoughts and suggestions which occurred to him on
the road are afterwards worked up into papers for the
Spectator.

When Addison landed in France in 1699, the power of
Louis XIV., so long the determined enemy of the English Revolution of 1688, had passed its climax.   The
Peace of Ryswick, by which the hopes of the Jacobites
were finally demolished, was two years old.   The king,
disappointed in his dreams of boundless military glory,
had fallen into a fit of devotion, and Addison, arriving
from England, with a very imperfect knowledge of the
language, was astonished to find the whole of French
literature saturated with the royal taste.   " As for the
state of learning," says he in a letter to Montague, dated
August 1699, " there is no book comes out at present
that has not something in it of an air of devotion.
Dacier has bin forced to prove his Plato a very good
Christian before he ventures upon his translation, and
has so far comply'd with ye tast of the age, that his
whole book is overrun with texts of Scripture, and y^e
notion of præ-existence, supposed to be stolen from two
verses of ye prophets.   Nay, ye humour is grown so universal that it is got among ye poets, who are every day
publishing Lives of Saints and Legends in Rhime."

Finding, perhaps, that the conversation at the capital
was not very congenial to his taste, he seems to have
hurried on to Blois, a town then noted for the purity
with which its inhabitants spoke the French language,
and where he had determined to make his temporary
abode.   His only record of his first impressions of Paris
is a casual criticism of " ye King's Statue that is lately

set up in the Place Vendôme." He visited, however,
both Versailles and Fontainebleau, and the preference
which he gives to the latter (in a letter to Congreve) is
interesting, as anticipating that taste for natural, as
opposed to artificial beauty, which he afterwards expressed in the *Spectator*.

"I don't believe, as good a poet as you are, that you can
make finer Lanskips than those about the King's houses, or
with all yor descriptions build a more magnificent palace than
Versailles.   I am, however, so singular as to prefer Fontainebleau to the rest.   It is situated among rocks and woods that
give you a fine variety of Savage prospects.   The King has
Humoured the Genius of the place, and only made of so much
art as is necessary to Help and regulate Nature, without reform-
ing her too much.   The Cascades seem to break through the
Clefts and cracks of Rocks that are covered over with Moss,
and look as if they were piled upon one another by Accident.   There is an artificial wildness in the Meadows, Walks,
and Canals, and ye Garden, instead of a Wall, is Fenced on the
Lower End by a Natural Mound of Rock-work that strikes the
eye very agreeably.   For my part, I think there is something
more charming in these rude heaps of Stone than in so many
Statues, and wou'd as soon see a River winding through Woods
and Meadows as when it is tossed up in such a variety of
figures at Versailles." [1]

Here and there, too, his correspondence exhibits traces
of that delicate vein of ridicule in which he is without
a rival, as in the following inimitable description of Le
Brun's paintings at Versailles :—

"The painter has represented his most Xtian Majesty

---

[1] Compare *Spectator* 414.   "I do not know whether I am singular
in my opinion, but for my part I would rather look upon a tree in
all its luxuriancy and diffusion of boughs and branches, rather
than when it is thus cut and trimmed into a mathematical figure ;
and cannot but fancy that an orchard in flower looks infinitely more
delightful than all the little labyrinths of the finished parterre."

under ye figure of Jupiter throwing thunderbolts all about
the ceiling, and striking terror into ye Danube and Rhine,
that lie astonished and blasted a little above the Cornice."

Of his life at Blois a very slight sketch has been preserved
by the Abbe Philippeaux, one of the many gossipping
informants from whom Spence collected his anecdotes :—

"Mr. Addison stayed above a year at Blois. He would
rise as early as between two and three in summer, and lie
abed till between eleven and twelve in the depth of winter.
He was untalkative while here, and often thoughtful; sometimes so lost in thought that I have come into his room and
have stayed five minutes there before he has known anything
of it. He had his masters generally at supper with him,
kept very little company beside, and had no amour whilst
here that I know of, and I think I should have known it if
he had had any."

The following characteristic letter to a gentleman of
Blois, with whom he seems to have had an altercation, is
interesting as showing the mixture of coolness and
dignity, the "blood and judgment well commingled"
which Hamlet praised in Horatio, and which are conspicuous in all Addison's actions, as well as in his
writings :—

"Sir,—I am always as slow in making an Enemy as a
Friend, and am therefore very ready to come to an Accom-
modation with you ; but as for any satisfaction, I don't think
it is due on either side when ye Affront is mutual. You
know very well that according to ye opinion of ye world a
man would as soon be called a Knave as a fool, and I believe
most people w^d be rather thought to want Legs than Brains.
But I suppose whatever we said in ye heat of discourse is not
ye real opinion we have of each other, since otherwise you
would have scorned to subscribe yourself as I do at present,
S^r, y^r very, etc.

A. Monsr L'Espagnol,
    Blois, 10^{br} 1699.

The length of Addison's sojourn at Blois seems to have been partly caused by the difficulty he experienced, owing to the defectiveness of his memory, in mastering the language. Finding himself at last able to converse easily, he returned to Paris some time in the autumn of 1700, in order to see a little of polite society there before starting on his travels in Italy. He found the best company in the capital among the men of letters, and he makes especial mention of Malebranche, whom he describes as solicitous about the adequate rendering of his works into English; and of Boileau, who, having now survived almost all his literary friends, seems, in his conversation with Addison, to have been even more than usually splenetic in his judgments on his contemporaries. The old poet and critic was, however, propitiated with the present of the *Musæ Anglicanæ;* and, according to Tickell, said "that he did not question there were excellent compositions in the native language of a country that possessed the Roman genius in so eminent a degree."

In general, Addison's remarks on the French character are not complimentary. He found the vanity of the people so elated by the elevation of the Duke of Anjou to the throne of Spain that they were insupportable, and he felt no reluctance to quit France for Italy. His observations on the national manners, as seen at Blois, are characteristic :—

"Truly by what I have yet seen, they are the Happiest nation in the world. 'Tis not in the pow'r of Want or Slavery to make 'em miserable. There is nothing to be met with in the Country but Mirth and Poverty. Ev'ry one sings, laughs, and starves. Their Conversation is generally Agreeable ; for if they have any Wit or Sense they are sure to show it. They never mend upon a Second meeting, but

use all the freedom and familiarity at first Sight that a long
Intimacy or Abundance of wine can scarce draw from an
Englishman.   Their Women are perfect Mistresses in this
Art of showing themselves to the best Advantage.   They are
always gay and sprightly, and set off ye worst faces in Europe
with ye best airs.   Ev'ry one knows how to give herself as
charming a look and posture as Sr Godfrey Kneller cd draw
her in." [1]

He embarked from Marseilles for Genoa in December
1700, having as his companion Edward Wortley Montague, whom Pope satirises under the various names of
Shylock, Worldly, and Avidien.   It is unnecessary to
follow him step by step in his travels, but the reader of
his *Letter to Lord Halifax* may still enjoy the delight and
enthusiasm to which he gives utterance on finding himself among the scenes described in his favourite authors:—

> " Poetic fields encompass me around,
>   And still I seem to tread on classic ground ;
>   For here the Muse so oft her harp has strung,
>   That not a mountain rears its head unsung ;
>   Renowned in verse each shady thicket grows,
>   And every stream in heavenly numbers flows." [2]

The phrase "classic ground," which has become pro-
verbial, is first used in these verses, and, as will have
been observed, Pope repeats it with evident reference to
the above passage in his satire on the travels of the
"young Æneas."   Addison seems to have carried the
Latin poets with him, and his quotations from them are
abundant and apposite.   When he is driven into the
harbour at Monaco, he remembers Lucan's description of
its safety and shelter ; as he passes under Monte Circeo,

---

[1] Letter to the Right Honourable Charles Montague, Esq.,
Blois, 10br 1699.

[2] Letter from Italy to Lord Halifax.

he feels that Virgil's description of Æneas' voyage by
the same spot can never be sufficiently admired ; he
recalls, as he crosses the Apennines, the fine lines of
Claudian recording the march of Honorius from Ravenna
to Rome ; and he delights to think that at the falls of
the Velino he can still see the "angry goddess" of the
Æneid (Alecto) "thus sinking, as it were, in a tempest,
and plunging herself into Hell " amidst such a scene of
horror and confusion.

His enthusiastic appreciation of the classics, which
caused him in judging any work of art to look in
the first place for regularity of design and simplicity of
effect, shows itself characteristically in his remarks on
the Lombard and German styles of architecture in Italy.
Of Milan Cathedral he speaks without much admiration,
but he was impressed with the wonders of the Certosa
near Pavia.   "I saw," says he, "between Pavia and
Milan the convent of the Carthusians, which is very
spacious and beautiful.   Their church is very fine and
curiously adorned, *but* of a Gothic structure."   His most
interesting criticism, however, is that on the Duomo at
Siena :—

"When a man sees the prodigious pains and expense that
our forefathers have been at in these barbarous buildings, one
cannot but fancy to himself what miracles of architecture they
would have left us had they only been instructed in the right
way, for when the devotion of those ages was much warmer than
that of the present, and the riches of the people much more at
the disposal of the priests, there was so much money consumed
on these Gothic cathedrals as would have finished a greater
variety of noble buildings than have been raised either before
or since that time.   One would wonder to see the vast labour
that has been laid out on this single cathedral.   The very spouts
are loaden with ornaments, the windows are formed like so

E

many scenes of perspective, with a multitude of little pillars
retiring behind one another, the great columns are finely en-
graven with fruits and foliage, that run twisting about them
from the very top to the bottom; the whole body of the church
is chequered with different lays of black and white marble, the
pavement curiously cut out in designs and Scripture stories,
and the front covered with such a variety of figures, and
overrun with so many mazes and little labyrinths of sculpture,
that nothing in the world can make a prettier show to those
who prefer false beauties and *affected ornaments* to a noble
and majestic simplicity." [1]

Addison had not reached that large liberality in
criticism afterwards attained by Sir Joshua Reynolds,
who, while insisting that in all art there was but *one*
true style, nevertheless allowed very high merit to what
he called the *characteristic* styles.   Sir Joshua would
never have fallen into the error of imputing affectation
to such simple and honest workmen as the early archi-
tects of Northern Italy.   The effects of Addison's classical
training are also very visible in his descriptions of natural
scenery.   There is in these nothing of that craving melancholy produced by a sense of the infinity of nature which
came into vogue after the French Revolution; no pro-
jection of the feelings of the spectator into the external
scene on which he gazes; nor, on the other hand, is
there any attempt to rival the art of the painter by presenting a landscape in words instead of in colours.   He
looks on nature with the same clear sight as the Greek
and Roman writers, and in describing a scene he selects
those particulars in it which he thinks best adapted to
arouse pleasurable images in the mind of the reader.
Take, for instance, the following excellent description of
his passage over the Apennines :—

[1] Addison's *Works* (Tickell's edition), vol. v. p. 301.

"The fatigue of our crossing the Apennines, and of our whole journey from Loretto to Rome, was very agreeably relieved by the variety of scenes we passed through. For, not to mention the rude prospect of rocks rising one above another, of the deep gutters worn in the sides of them by torrents of rain and snow-water, or the long channels of sand winding about their bottoms, that are sometimes filled with so many rivers : we saw in six days' travelling the several seasons of the year in their beauty and perfection. We were sometimes shivering on the top of a bleak mountain, and a little while afterwards basking in a warm valley, covered with violets and almond trees in blossom, the bees already swarming over them, though but in the month of February. Sometimes our road led us through groves of olives, or by gardens of oranges, or into several hollow apartments among the rocks and mountains, that look like so many natural greenhouses ; as being always shaded with a great variety of trees and shrubs that never lose their verdure." [1]

Though his thoughts during his travels were largely occupied with objects chiefly interesting to his taste and imagination, and though he busied himself with such compositions as the *Epistle from Italy*, the *Dialogue on Medals*, and the first four acts of *Cato*, he did not forget that his experience was intended to qualify him for taking part in the affairs of State. And when he reached Geneva, in December 1701, the door to a political career seemed to be on the point of opening. He there learned, as Tickell informs us, that he had been selected to attend the army under Prince Eugene as secretary from the King. He accordingly waited in the city for official confirmation of this intelligence ; but his hopes were doomed to disappointment. William III. died in March 1702 ; Halifax, on whom Addison's prospects chiefly depended, was struck off the Privy Council by Queen Anne ; and

[1] Addison's *Works* (Tickell's edition), vol. v. p. 213.

the travelling pension ceased with the life of the sovereign who had granted it. Henceforth he had to trust to his own resources, and though the loss of his pension does not seem to have compelled him at once to turn homewards, as he continued on his route to Vienna, yet an incident that occurred towards the close of his travels shows that he was prepared to eke out his income by undertaking work that would have been naturally irksome to him.

At Rotterdam, on his return towards England, he met with Jacob Tonson, the bookseller, for whom, as has been said, he had already done some work as a translator. Tonson was one of the founders of the Kit-Kat Club, and in that capacity was brought into frequent and intimate connection with the Whig magnates of the day. Among these was the Duke of Somerset, who, through his wife, then high in Queen Anne's favour, exercised considerable influence on the course of affairs. The Duke required a tutor for his son, Lord Hertford, and Tonson recommended Addison. On the Duke's approval of the recommendation, the bookseller seems to have communicated with Addison, who expressed himself in general terms as willing to undertake the charge of Lord Hertford, but desired to know more particulars about his engagement. These were furnished by the Duke in a letter to Tonson, and they are certainly a very curious illustration of the manners of the period. "I ought," says his Grace, "to enter into that affair more freely and more plainly, and tell you what I propose, and what I hope he will comply with— viz. I desire he may be more on the account of a companion in my son's travels than as a governor, and that

as such I shall account him : my meaning is that neither
lodging, travelling, nor diet shall cost him sixpence, and
over and above that, my son shall present him at the
year's end with a hundred guineas, as long as he is pleased
to continue in that service to my son, by his personal
attendance and advice, in what he finds necessary during
his time of travelling."

To this not very tempting proposal Addison replied :
"I have lately received one or two advantageous offers
of ye same nature, but as I should be very ambitious of
executing any of your Grace's commands, so I can't think
of taking ye like employ from any other hands.   As for
ye recompense that is proposed to me, I must take the
liberty to assure your Grace that I should not see my
account in it, but in ye hope that I have to recommend
myself to your Grace's favour and approbation."   This
reply proved highly offensive to the Duke, who seems
to have considered his own offer a magnificent one.
"Your letter of the 16th," he writes to Tonson on June
22, 1703, "with one from Mr. Addison, came safe to me.
You say he will give me an account of his readiness of
complying with my proposal.   I will set down his own
words, which are thus : 'As for the recompense that is
proposed to me, I must confess I can by no means see
my account in it,' etc.   All the other parts of his letter
are compliments to me, which he thought he was bound
in good breeding to write, and as such I have taken them,
and no otherwise ; and now I leave you to judge how
ready he is to comply with my proposal.   Therefore I
have wrote by this first post to prevent his coming to
England on my account, and have told him plainly that I
must look for another, which I cannot be long a-finding."

Addison's principal biographer, Miss Aikin, expresses great contempt for the niggardliness of the Duke, and says that "Addison must often have congratulated himself in the sequel on that exertion of proper spirit by which he had escaped from wasting in an attendance little better than servile three precious years, which he found means of employing so much more to his own honour and satisfaction, and to the advantage of the public." Mean as the Duke's offer was, it is nevertheless plain that Addison really intended to accept it, and, this being so, he can scarcely be congratulated on having on this occasion displayed his usual tact and felicity. Two courses appear to have been open to him. He might either have simply declined the offer "as not finding his account in it," or he might have accepted it in view of the future advantages which he hoped to derive from the Duke's "favour and approbation," in which case he should have said nothing about finding the "recompense" proposed insufficient. By the course that he took he contrived to miss an appointment which he seems to have made up his mind to accept, and he offended an influential statesman whose favour he was anxious to secure.

To his pecuniary embarrassments was soon added domestic loss. At Amsterdam he received news of his father's death, and it may be supposed that the private business in which he must have been involved in consequence of this event brought him to England, where he arrived some time in the autumn of 1703.

CHAPTER IV.

ADDISON'S fortunes were now at their lowest ebb. The party from which he had looked for preferment was out of office ; his chief political patron was in particular discredit at Court ; his means were so reduced that he was forced to adopt a style of living not much more splendid than that of the poorest inhabitants of Grub Street. Yet within three years of his return to England he was promoted to be an Under-Secretary of State, a post from which he mounted to one position of honour after another till his final retirement from political life. That he was able to take advantage of the opportunity that offered itself was owing to his own genius and capacity; the opportunity was the fruit of circumstances which had produced an entire revolution in the position of English men of letters.

Through the greater part of Charles II.'s reign the profession of literature was miserably degraded. It is true that the King himself, a man of wit and taste, was not slow in his appreciation of art; but he was by his character insensible to what was serious or elevated, and the poetry of gallantry, which he preferred, was quite within reach of the courtiers by whom he was surrounded.

Rochester, Buckingham, Sedley, and Dorset are among
the principal poetical names of the period; all of them
being well qualified to shine in verse, the chief require-
ments of which were a certain grace of manner, an air
of fashionable breeding, and a complete disregard of the
laws of decency.   Besides these "songs by persons of
quality," the principal entertainment was provided by
the drama.   But the stage, seldom a lucrative profession,
was then crowded with writers whose fertile, if not very
lofty, invention kept down the price of plays.   Otway, the
most successful dramatist of his time, died in a state of
indigence, and as some say almost of starvation, while
playwrights of less ability, if the house was ill-attended
on the third night, when the poet received all the profits
of the performance, were forced, as Oldham says, "to
starve or live in tatters all the year." [1]

Periodical literature, in the shape of journals and
magazines, had as yet no existence ; nor could the satirical poet or the pamphleteer find his remuneration in
controversial writing, the strong reaction against Puritanism having raised the monarchy to a position in which
it was practically secure against the assaults of all its
enemies.   The author of the most brilliant satire of the
period, who had used all the powers of a rich imagination
to discredit the Puritan and Republican cause, was paid
with nothing more solid than admiration, and died
neglected and in want.

> " The wretch, at summing up his misspent days,
>   Found nothing left but poverty and praise !
>   Of all his gains by verse he could not save
>   Enough to purchase flannel and a grave !

---

[1] Oldham's Satire *Dissuading from Poetry.*

> Reduced to want he in due time fell sick,
> Was fain to die, and be interred on tick;
> And well might bless the fever that was sent
> To rid him hence, and his worse fate prevent." [1]

In the latter part of this reign, however, a new combination of circumstances produced a great change in the character of English literature and in the position of its professors. The struggle of Parties recommenced. Wearied with the intolerable rule of the Saints, the nation had been at first glad to leave its newly-restored King to his pleasures, but, as the memories of the Commonwealth became fainter, the people watched with a growing feeling of disgust the selfishness and extravagance of the Court, while the scandalous sale of Dunkirk and the sight of the Dutch fleet on the Thames made them think of the patriotic energies which Cromwell had succeeded in arousing.   At the same time the thinly-disguised inclination of the King to Popery, and the avowed opinions of his brother, raised a general feeling of alarm for the Protestant liberties of the nation.   On the other hand, the Puritans, taught moderation by adversity, exhibited the really religious side of their character, and attracted towards themselves a considerable portion of the aristocracy, as well as of the commercial and professional classes in the metropolis—a combination of interests which helped to form the nucleus of the Whig party. The clergy and the landed proprietors, who had been the chief sufferers from Parliamentary rule, naturally adhered to the Court, and were nicknamed by their opponents Tories.   Violent party conflicts ensued, marked by such incidents as the Test Act, the Exclusion Bill, the intrigues

[1] Oldham's Satire *Dissuading from Poetry.*

of Monmouth, the Popish Plot, and the trial and acquittal
of Shaftesbury on the charge of high treason.

Finding his position no longer so easy as at his restoration, Charles naturally bethought him of calling literature to his assistance. The stage, being completely
under his control, seemed the readiest instrument for his
purpose ; the order went forth ; and an astonishing dis-
play of monarchical fervour in all the chief dramatists
of the time—Otway, Dryden, Lee, and Crowne—was the
result. Shadwell, who was himself inclined to the Whig
interest, laments the change:

> " The stage, like old Rump pulpits, is become
> The scene of News, a furious Party's drum.

But the political influence of the drama and the audience
to which it appealed being necessarily limited, the King
sought for more powerful literary artillery, and he found
it in the serviceable genius of Dryden, whose satirical and
controversial poems date from this period. The wide
popularity of *Absalom and Achitophel*, written against
Monmouth and Shaftesbury ; of *The Medal*, satirising the
acquittal of Shaftesbury; of *The Hind and Panther*, composed to advance the Romanising projects of James II. ;
points to the vast influence exercised by literature in the
party struggle. Nevertheless, in spite of all that Dryden
had done for the Royal cause, in spite of the fact that he
himself had more than once appealed to the poet for
assistance, the ingratitude or levity of Charles was so
inveterate that he let the poet's services go almost un-
requited. Dryden, it is true, held the posts of Laureate
and Royal Historiographer, but his salary was always in
arrears, and the letter which he addressed to Rochester,

First Lord of the Treasury, asking for six months' payment of what was due to him tells its own story.

James II. cared nothing for literature, and was probably too dull of apprehension to understand the incalculable service that Dryden had rendered to his cause. He showed his appreciation of the Poet-Laureate's genius by deducting £100 from the salary which his brother had promised him, and by cutting off from the emoluments of the office the time-honoured butt of canary !

Under William III. the complexion of affairs again altered. The Court, in the old sense of the word, ceased to be a paramount influence in literature. William III. derived his authority from Parliament; he knew that he must support it mainly by his sword and his statesmanship. A stranger to England, its manners and its language, he showed little disposition to encourage letters. Pope, indeed, maliciously suggests that he had the bad taste to admire the poetry of Blackmore, whom he knighted; but, as a matter of fact, the honour was conferred on the worthy Sir Richard in consequence of his distinction in medicine, and he himself bears witness to William's contempt for poetry.

> " Reverse of Louis he, example rare,
> Loved to deserve the praise he could not bear.
> He shunned the acclamations of the throng,
> And always coldly heard the poet's song.
> Hence the great King the Muses did neglect,
> And the mere poet met with small respect." [1]

Such political verse as we find in this reign generally consists, like Halifax's *Epistle to Lord Dorset*, or Addison's own *Address to King William*, of hyperbolical

---

[1] Blackmore, *The Kit-Kats.*

flattery. Opposition was extinct, for both parties had for the moment united to promote the Revolution, and the only discordant notes amid the chorus of adulation proceeded from Jacobite writers concealed in the garrets and cellars of Grub Street. Such an atmosphere was not favourable to the production of literature of an elevated or even of a characteristic order.

Addison's return to England coincided most happily with another remarkable turn of the tide. Leaning decidedly to the Tory party, who were now strongly leavened with the Jacobite element, Anne had not long succeeded to the throne before she seized an opportunity for dismissing the Whig Ministry whom she found in possession of office. The Whigs, equally alarmed at the influence acquired by their rivals, and at the danger which threatened the Protestant succession, neglected no effort to counterbalance the loss of their sovereign's favour by strengthening their credit with the people. Having been trained in a school which had at least qualified them to appreciate the influence of style, the aristocratic leaders of the party were well aware of the advantages they would derive by attracting to themselves the services of the ablest writers of the day. Hence they made it their policy to mingle with men of letters on an equal footing, and to hold out to them an expectation of a share in the advantages to be reaped from the overthrow of their rivals.

The result of this union of forces was a great increase in the number of literary-political clubs. In its half-aristocratic, half-democratic constitution, the club was the natural product of enlarged political freedom, and helped to extend the organisation of polite opinion beyond the narrow orbit of Court society. Addison himself, in his simple style, points out the nature of the fundamental principle of Association which he observed in operation all around him. " When a set of men find themselves agree in any particular, though never so trivial, they establish themselves into a kind of fraternity, and meet once or twice a week upon the account of such a fantastic resemblance."[1] Among these societies, in the first years of the eighteenth century, the most celebrated was perhaps the Kit-Kat Club. It consisted of thirty-nine of the leading men of the Whig party; and, though many of these were of the highest rank, it is a characteristic fact that the founder of the club should have been the bookseller Jacob Tonson. It was probably through his influence, joined to that of Halifax, that Addison was elected a member of the society soon after his return to England. Among its prominent members was the Duke of Somerset, the first meeting between whom and Addison, after the correspondence that had passed between them, must have been somewhat embarrassing. The club assembled at one Christopher Catt's, a pastry-cook, who gave his name both to the society and the mutton-pies which were its ordinary entertainment. Each member was compelled to select a lady as his toast, and the verses which he composed in her honour were engraved on the wine-glasses belonging to the club. Addison chose the Countess of Manchester, whose acquaintance he had made in Paris, and complimented her in the following lines :—

> " While haughty Gallia's dames, that spread
> O'er their pale cheeks an artful red,

---

[1] *Spectator*, No. 9.

> Beheld this beauteous stranger there,
> In native charms divinely fair,
> Confusion in their looks they showed,
> And with unborrowed blushes glowed."

Circumstances seemed now to be conspiring in favour
of the Whigs. The Tories, whose strength lay mainly
in the Jacobite element, were jealous of Marlborough's
ascendency over the Queen; on the other hand, the
Duchess of Marlborough, who was rapidly acquiring the
chief place in Anne's affections, intrigued in favour of
the opposite faction. In spite, too, of her Tory predilec-
tions, the Queen, finding her throne menaced by the
ambition of Louis XIV., was compelled in self-defence
to look for support to the party which had most vigorously identified itself with the principles of the Revolution. She bestowed her unreserved confidence on
Marlborough, and he, in order to counterbalance the
influence of the Jacobites, threw himself into the arms
of the Whigs. Being named Captain-General in 1704,
he undertook the campaign which he brought to so
glorious a conclusion on the 2d of August in that year
at the battle of Blenheim.

Godolphin, who in the absence of Marlborough
occupied the chief place in the Ministry, moved perhaps
by patriotic feeling, and no doubt also by a sense of the
advantage which his party would derive from this great
victory, was anxious that it should be commemorated
in adequate verse. He accordingly applied to Halifax
as the person to whom the *sacer vates* required for the
occasion would probably be known. Halifax has had
the misfortune to have his character transmitted to
posterity by two poets who hated him either on public or

private grounds. Swift describes him as the would-be
"Mæcenas of the nation," but insinuates that he
neglected the wants of the poets whom he patronised :

> " Himself as rich as fifty Jews,
>   Was easy though they wanted shoes."

Pope also satirises the vanity and meanness of his
disposition in the well-known character of Bufo. Such
portraits, though they are justified to some extent by
evidence coming from other quarters, are not to be too
strictly examined as if they bore the stamp of historic
truth. It is, at any rate, certain that Halifax always
proved himself a warm and zealous friend to Addison,
and when Godolphin applied to him for a poet to cele-
brate Blenheim, he answered that, though acquainted
with a person who possessed every qualification for the
task, he could not ask him to undertake it. Being
pressed for his reasons, he replied "that while too
many fools and blockheads were maintained in their
pride and luxury at the public expense, such men as
were really an honour to their age and country were
shamefully suffered to languish in obscurity; that, for
his own share, he would never desire any gentleman of
parts and learning to employ his time in celebrating a
Ministry who had neither the justice nor the generosity
to make it worth his while." In answer to this the
Lord Treasurer assured Halifax that any person whom
he might name as equal to the required task, should have
no cause to repent of having rendered his assistance ;
whereupon Halifax mentioned Addison, but stipulated
that all advances to the latter must come from Godolphin himself. Accordingly Boyle, Chancellor of the
Exchequer, afterwards Lord Carleton, was despatched

on the embassy, and, if Pope is to be trusted, found
Addison lodged up three pair of stairs over a small
shop.   He opened to him the subject, and informed him
that, in return for the service that was expected of him,
he was instructed to offer him a Commissionership of
Appeal in the Excise, as a pledge of more considerable
advancement in the future.   The fruits of this negotia-
tion were *The Campaign.*

Warton disposes of the merits of *The Campaign* with
the cavalier criticism, so often since repeated, that it is
merely "a gazette in rhyme."   In one sense the judgment is no doubt just.   As a poem, *The Campaign* shows
neither loftiness of invention nor enthusiasm of personal
feeling, and it cannot therefore be ranked with such an
ode as Horace's *Qualem ministrum,* or with Pope's very
fine *Epistle* to the Earl of Oxford after his disgrace.   Its
methodical narrative style is scarcely misrepresented by
Warton's sarcastic description of it; but it should be
remembered that this style was adopted by Addison
with deliberate intention.   " Thus," says he, in the conclusion of the poem,

> " Thus would I fain Britannia's wars rehearse
>   In the smooth records of a faithful verse;
>   That, if such numbers can o'er time prevail,
>   May tell posterity the wondrous tale.
>   When actions unadorned are faint and weak
>   Cities and countries must be taught to speak;
>   Gods may descend in factions from the skies,
>   And rivers from their oozy beds arise;
>   Fiction may deck the truth with spurious rays,
>   And round the hero cast a borrowed blaze.
>   Marlbro's exploits appear divinely bright,
>   And proudly shine in their own native light;
>   Raised in themselves their genuine charms they boast,
>   And those that paint them truest praise them most."

The design here avowed is certainly not poetical, but
it is eminently business-like and extremely well adapted
to the end in view.   What Godolphin wanted was a set
of complimentary verses on Marlborough.   Addison,
with infinite tact, declares that the highest compliment
that can be paid to the hero is to recite his actions in
their unadorned grandeur.   This happy turn of flattery
shows how far he had advanced in literary skill since he
wrote his address *To the King*.   He had then excused
himself for the inadequate celebration of William's
deeds on the plea that, great though these might be,
they were too near the poet's own time to be seen in
proper focus.   A thousand years hence, he suggests,
some Homer may be inspired by the theme "and Boyne
be sung when it has ceased to flow."   This could not
have been very consolatory to a mortal craving for contemporary applause, and the apology offered in *The
Campaign* for the prosaic treatment of the subject is far
more dexterous.   Bearing in mind the fact that it was
written to order, and that the poet deliberately declined
to avail himself of the aid of fiction, we must allow
that the construction of the poem exhibits both art and
dignity.   The allusion to the vast slaughter at Blenheim
in the opening paragraph—

> " Rivers of blood I see and hills of slain,
>   An Iliad rising out of one campaign "—

is not very fortunate ; but the lines describing the ambition of Louis XIV. are weighty and dignified, and
the couplet indicating through the single image of the
Danube the vast extent of the French encroachments
shows how thoroughly Addison was imbued with the
spirit of classical poetry :

F

> " The rising Danube its long race began,
>   And half its course through the new conquests ran."

With equal felicity he describes the position and intervention of England, seizing at the same time the opportunity for a panegyric on her free institutions :

> "Thrice happy Britain from the kingdoms rent
>   To sit the guardian of the Continent !
>   That sees her bravest sons advanced so high
>   And flourishing so near her prince's eye ;
>   Thy favourites grow not up by fortune's sport,
>   Or from the crimes and follies of a court:
>   On the firm basis of desert they rise,
>   From long-tried faith and friendship's holy ties,
>   Their sovereign's well-distinguished smiles they share,
>   Her ornaments in peace, her strength in war ;
>   The nation thanks them with a public voice,
>   By showers of blessings Heaven approves their choice ;
>   Envy itself is dumb, in wonder lost,
>   And factions strive who shall applaud them most."

He proceeds in a stream of calm and equal verse, enlivened by dexterous allusions and occasional happy
turns of expression to describe the scenery of the
Moselle ; the march between the Maese and the Danube ; the heat to which the army was exposed ; the
arrival on the Neckar ; and the track of devastation left
by the French armies.   The meeting between Marlborough and Eugene inspires him again to raise his
style :

> " Great souls by instinct to each other turn,
>   Demand alliance, and in friendship burn,
>   A sudden friendship, while with outstretched rays
>   They meet each other mingling blaze with blaze.
>   Polished in courts, and hardened in the field,
>   Renowned for conquest, and in council skilled,

> Their courage dwells not in a troubled flood
> Of mounting spirits and fermenting blood;
> Lodged in the soul, with virtue overruled,
> Inflamed by reason, and by reason cooled,
> In hours of peace content to be unknown
> And only in the field of battle shown;
> To souls like these in mutual friendship joined
> Heaven dares entrust the cause of human kind."

The celebrated passage describing Marlborough's conduct at Blenheim is certainly the finest in the poem:

> " 'Twas then great Marlborough's mighty soul was proved
> That in the shock of charging hosts unmoved,
> Amidst confusion, horror, and despair
> Examined all the dreadful scenes of war;
> In peaceful thought the field of death surveyed,
> To fainting squadrons sent the timely aid,
> Inspired repulsed battalions to engage,
> And taught the doubtful battle where to rage.
> So when an angel by divine command
> With rising tempests shakes a guilty land,
> Such as of late o'er pale Britannia past,
> Calm and serene he drives the furious blast;
> And pleased th' Almighty's orders to perform,
> Rides in the whirlwind and directs the storm."

Johnson makes some characteristic criticisms on this simile, which indeed, he maintains, is not a simile, but "an exemplification." He says: "Marlborough is so like the angel in the poem that the action of both is almost the same, and performed by both in the same manner. Marlborough 'teaches the battle to rage;' the angel 'directs the storm;' Marlborough is 'unmoved in peaceful thought;' the angel is 'calm and serene;' Marlborough stands 'unmoved amid the shock of hosts;' the angel rides 'calm in the whirlwind.' The lines on Marlborough are just and noble; but the simile gives almost the same images a second time."

This judgment would be unimpeachable if the force of the simile lay solely in the likeness between Marlborough and the angel, but it is evident that equal stress is to be laid on the resemblance between the battle and the storm. It was Addison's intention to raise in the mind of the reader the noblest possible idea of composure and design in the midst of confusion : to do this he selected an angel as the minister of the divine purpose, and a storm as the symbol of fury and devastation; and, in order to heighten his effect, he recalls with true art the violence of the particular tempest which had recently ravaged the country. Johnson has noticed the close similarity between the persons of Marlborough and the angel ; but he has exaggerated the resemblance between the actions in which they are severally engaged.

The Campaign completely fulfilled the purpose for which it was written. It strengthened the position of the Whig Ministry, and secured for its author the advancement that had been promised him. Early in 1706 Addison, on the recommendation of Lord Godolphin, was promoted from the Commissionership of Appeals in Excise to be Under-Secretary of State to Sir Charles Hedges. The latter was one of the few Tories who had retained their position in the Ministry since the restoration of the Whigs to the favour of their sovereign, and he, too, shortly vanished from the stage like his more distinguished friends, making way for the Earl of Sunderland, a staunch Whig, and son-in-law to the Duke of Marlborough.

Addison's duties as Under-Secretary were probably not particularly arduous.   In 1705 he was permitted to attend Lord Halifax to the Court of Hanover, whither the latter was sent to carry the Act for the Naturalisation of the Electress Sophia.   The mission also included Vanbrugh, who, as Clarencieux King-at-Arms, was charged to invest the Elector with the Order of the Garter; the party thus constituted affording a remarkable illustration of the influence exercised by literature over the politics of the period.   Addison must have obtained during this journey considerable insight into the nature of England's foreign policy, as, besides establishing the closest relations with Hanover, Halifax was also instructed to form an alliance with the United Provinces for securing the succession of the House of Brunswick to the English throne.

In the meantime his imagination was not idle. After helping Steele in the composition of his *Tender Husband*, which was acted in 1705, he found time for engaging in a fresh literary enterprise of his own.   The principles of operatic music, which had long been developed in Italy, had been slow in making their way to this country.   Their introduction had been delayed partly by the French prejudices of Charles II., but more perhaps by the strong insular tastes of the people and by the vigorous forms of the native drama. What the untutored English audience liked best to hear was a well-marked tune sung in a fine natural way : the kind of music which was in vogue on the stage till the end of the seventeenth century was simply the regular drama interspersed with airs ; *recitative* was unknown ; and there was no attempt to culti-

vate the voice according to the methods practised in
the Italian schools.   But with the increase of wealth
and travel more exacting tastes began to prevail : Italian
singers appeared on the stage and exhibited to the audience capacities of voice of which they had hitherto had
no experience.   In 1705 was acted at the Haymarket
Arsinoe, the first opera constructed in England on
avowedly Italian principles.   The words were still in
English, but the dialogue was throughout in *recitative*.
The composer was Thomas Clayton, who, though a man
entirely devoid of genius, had travelled in Italy, and was
eager to turn to account the experience which he had
acquired.   In spite of its badness *Arsinoe* greatly impressed the public taste ; and it was soon followed by
Camilla, a version of an opera by Bononcini, portions of
which were sung in Italian and portions in English, an
absurdity on which Addison justly comments in a
number of the *Spectator*.   His remarks on the consequences of translating the Italian operas are equally
humorous and just.

" As there was no great danger," says he, " of hurting the
sense of these extraordinary pieces, our authors would often
make words of their own which were entirely foreign to the
meaning of the passages they pretended to translate ; their
chief care being to make the numbers of the English verse
answer to those of the Italian, that both of them might go
to the same tune.   Thus the famous song in *Camilla :*

'Barbara si t'intendo,' etc.
'Barbarous woman, yes, I know your meaning.'

which expresses the resentment of an angry lover, was translated into that English lamentation—

'Frail are a lover's hopes,' etc.

And it was pleasant enough to see the most refined persons

of the British nation dying away and languishing to notes
that were filled with the spirit of rage and indignation.   It
happened also very frequently where the sense was rightly
translated, the necessary transposition of words, which were
drawn out of the phrase of one tongue into that of another,
made the music appear very absurd in one tongue that was
very natural in the other.   I remember an Italian verse
that ran thus, word for word :

'And turned my rage into pity,

which the English for rhyme's sake translated,

'And into pity turned my rage.'

By this means the soft notes that were adapted to pity in
the Italian fell upon the word 'rage' in the English ; and
the angry sounds that were turned to rage in the original
were made to express pity in the translation.   It oftentimes
happened likewise that the finest notes in the air fell upon
the most insignificant word in the sentence.   I have known
the word 'and' pursued through the whole gamut ; have
been entertained with many a melodious 'the ; ' and have
heard the most beautiful graces, quavers, and divisions bestowed upon 'then,' 'for,' and 'from,' to the eternal honour
of our English particles." [1]

Perceiving these radical defects, Addison seems to
have been ambitious of showing by example how they
might be remedied.   "The great success this opera
(*Arsinoe*) met with produced," says he, "some attempts
of forming pieces upon Italian plans, which should give
a more natural and reasonable entertainment than what
can be met with in the elaborate trifles of that nation.
This alarmed the poetasters and fiddlers of the town,
who were used to deal in a more ordinary kind of ware ;
and therefore laid down an established rule, which is
received as such to this day, 'That nothing is capable
of being well set to music that is not nonsense.'" [2]   The

[1] *Spectator*, No. 18.   [2] *Ibid.*

allusion to the failure of the writer's own opera of *Rosamond* is unmistakable. The piece was performed on the 2d of April 1706, but was coldly received, and after two or three representations was withdrawn.

The reasons which the *Spectator* assigns for the catastrophe betray rather the self-love of the author than the clear perception of the critic. *Rosamond* failed because, in the first place, it was very bad as a musical composition. Misled by the favour with which *Arsinoe* was received, Addison seems to have regarded Clayton as a great musician, and he put his poem into the hands of the latter, thinking that his score would be as superior to that of *Arisinoe* as his own poetry was to the words of that opera. Clayton, however, had no genius, and only succeeded in producing what Sir John Hawkins, quoting with approbation the words of another critic, calls "a confused chaos of music, the only merit of which is its shortness."[1]

But it may be doubted whether in any case the most skilful composer could have produced music of a high order adapted to the poetry of *Rosamond*. The play is neither a tragedy, a comedy, nor a melodrama. It seems that Eleanor did not really poison Fair Rosamond, but only administered to her a sleeping potion, and, as she takes care to explain to the King,

> "The bowl with drowsy juices filled,
> From cold Egyptian drugs distilled,
> In borrowed death has closed her eyes."

This information proves highly satisfactory to the King, not only because he is gratified to find that Rosamond is

[1] Sir John Hawkins' *History of Music*, vol. v. p. 137.

not dead, but also because, even before discovering her supposed dead body, he had resolved, in consequence of a dream sent to him by his guardian angel, to terminate the relations existing between them.   The Queen and he accordingly arrange in a business-like manner that Rosamond shall be quietly removed in her trance to a nunnery; a reconciliation is then effected between the husband and wife, who, as we are led to suppose, live happily ever after.

The main motive of the opera in Addison's mind appears to have been the desire of complimenting the Marlborough family.   It is dedicated to the Duchess; the warlike character of Henry naturally recalls the prowess of the great modern captain; and the King is consoled by his guardian angel for the loss of Fair Rosamond with a vision of the future glories of Blenheim :

> " To calm thy grief and lull thy cares
>   Look up and see
> What, after long revolving years,
>   Thy bower shall be !
> When time its beauties shall deface,
> And only with its ruins grace
> The future prospect of the place !
> Behold the glorious pile ascending,
> Columns swelling, arches bending,
> Domes in awful pomp arising,
> Art in curious strokes surprising,
> Foes in figured fights contending,
> Behold the glorious pile ascending."

This is graceful enough, but it scarcely offers material for music of a serious kind.   Nor can the Court have been greatly impressed by the compliment paid to its morality as contrasted with that of Charles II., conveyed

as it was by the mouth of Grideline, one or the comic
characters in the piece—

> " Since conjugal passion
> Is come into fashion,
> And marriage so blest on the throne is,
> Like a Venus I'll shine,
> Be fond and be fine,
> And Sir Trusty shall be my Adonis."

The ill success of *Rosamond* confirmed Addison's
dislike to the Italian opera, which he displayed both in
his grave and humorous papers on the subject in the
Spectator. The disquisition upon the various actors of
the lion in *Hydaspes* is one of his happiest inspirations;
but his serious criticisms are, as a rule, only just in so
far as they are directed against the dramatic absurdities
of the Italian opera. As to his technical qualifications
as a critic of music, it will be sufficient to cite the opinion
of Dr. Burney :—" To judges of music nothing more
need be said of Mr. Addison's abilities to decide con-
cerning the comparative degrees of national excellence
in the art, and the merit of particular masters, than his
predilection for the productions of Clayton and in-
sensibility to the force and originality of Handel's
compositions in *Rinaldo.*"[1]

In December 1708 the Earl of Sunderland was displaced
to make room for the Tory Lord Dartmouth, and Addison,
as Under-Secretary, following the fortunes of his superior,
found himself again without employment. Fortunately
for him the Earl of Wharton was almost immediately
afterwards made Lord-Lieutenant of Ireland, and offered
him the lucrative post of Secretary. The Earl, who was

[1] Burney's *History of Music,* vol. iv. p. 203.

subsequently created a Marquis, was the father of the famous Duke satirised in Pope's first *Moral Essay;* he was in every respect the opposite of Addison—a vehement Republican, a sceptic, unprincipled in his morals, venal in his methods of Government.   He was nevertheless a man of the finest talents, and seems to have possessed the power of gaining personal ascendency over his companions by a profound knowledge of character.   An acquaintance with Addison, doubtless commencing at the Kit-Kat Club, of which both were members, had convinced him that the latter had eminent qualifications for the task, which the Secretary's post would involve, of dealing with men of very various conditions.   Of the feelings with which Addison on his side regarded the Earl we have no record.   "It is reasonable to suppose," says Johnson, "that he counteracted, as far as he was able, the malignant and blasting influence of the Lieutenant; and that, at least, by his intervention some good was done and some mischief prevented."   Not a shadow of an imputation, at any rate, rests upon his own conduct as Secretary.   He appears to have acted strictly on that conception of public duty which he defines in one of his papers in the *Spectator.*   Speaking of the marks of a corrupt official, "Such an one," he declares, "is the man who upon any pretence whatsoever, receives more than what is the stated and unquestioned fee of his office. Gratifications, tokens of thankfulness, despatch money, and the like specious terms, are the pretences under which corruption very frequently shelters itself.   An honest man will, however, look on all these methods as unjustifiable, and will enjoy himself better in a moderate fortune that is gained with honour and reputation, than

in an overgrown estate that is cankered with the ac-
quisitions of rapine and exaction.   Were all our offices
discharged with such an inflexible integrity, we should
not see men in all ages, who grow up to exorbitant
wealth, with the abilities which are to be met with in an
ordinary mechanic." [1]   His friends perhaps considered
that his impartiality was somewhat overstrained, since he
always declined to remit the customary fees in their
favour.   "For," said he, "I may have forty friends,
whose fees may be two guineas a-piece; then I lose
eighty guineas, and my friends gain but two a-piece."

He took with him as his own Secretary, Eustace Budgell, who was related to him, and for whom he seems to
have felt a warm affection.   Budgell was a man of considerable literary ability, and was the writer of the various
papers in the *Spectator* signed "X.," some of which
succeed happily in imitating Addison's style.   While he
was under his friend's guidance his career was fairly
successful, but his temper was violent, and when, at a
later period of his life, he served in Ireland under a new
Lieutenant and another Secretary, he became involved
in disputes which led to his dismissal.   A furious pamphlet against the Lord-Lieutenant, the Duke of Bolton,
published by him in spite of Addison's remonstrances,
only complicated his position, and from this period his
fortunes steadily declined.   He lost largely in the South
Sea Scheme; spent considerable sums in a vain endeavour
to obtain a seat in Parliament; and at last came under
the influence of his kinsman, Tindal, the well-known
deist, whose will he is accused of having falsified.   With
his usual infelicity he happened to rouse the resentment

[1] *Spectator*, No. 469.

of Pope, and was treated in consequence to one of the deadly couplets with which that great poet was in the habit of repaying real or supposed injuries:

> "Let Budgell charge low Grub Street on his quill,
> And write whate'er he pleased,—except his will."

The lines were memorable, and were doubtless often quoted, and the wretched man finding his life insupportable, ended it by drowning himself in the Thames.

During his residence in Ireland Addison firmly cemented his friendship with Swift, whose acquaintance he had probably made after *The Campaign* had given him a leading position in the Whig party, on the side of which the sympathies of both were then enlisted. Swift's admiration for Addison was warm and generous. When the latter was on the point of embarking on his new duties, Swift wrote to a common friend, Colonel Hunter :— " Mr. Addison is hurrying away for Ireland, and I pray too much business may not spoil *le plus honnete homme du monde.*" To Archbishop King he wrote :—" Mr. Addison, who goes over our first secretary, is a most excellent person, and being my intimate friend I shall use all my credit to set him right in his notions of persons and things." Addison's duties took him occasionally to England, and during one of his visits Swift writes to him from Ireland :—" I am convinced that whatever Government come over you will find all marks of kindness from any parliament here with respect to your employment; the Tories contending with the Whigs which should speak best of you. In short, if you will come over again when you are at leisure we will raise an army and make you King of Ireland. Can you

think so meanly of a kingdom as not to be pleased that
every creature in it, who hath one grain of worth, has a
veneration for you?" In his *Journal to Stella* he says,
under date of October 12, 1710: "Mr. Addison's election has passed easy and undisputed; and I believe if
he had a mind to be chosen king he would hardly be
refused." On his side Addison's feelings were equally
warm. He presented Swift with a copy of his *Remarks
on Several Parts of Italy*, inscribing it—"To the most
agreeable companion, the truest friend, and the greatest
genius of his age."

This friendship, founded on mutual respect, was destined to be impaired by political differences. In 1710
the credit of the Whig Ministry had been greatly undermined by the combined craft of Harley and Mrs. Masham,
and Swift, who was anxious as to his position, on coming
over to England to press his claims on Somers and
Halifax, found that they were unable to help him. He
appears to have considered that their want of power
proceeded from want of will; at any rate, he made
advances to Harley, which were of course gladly received.
The Ministry were at this time being hard pressed by
the *Examiner*, under the conduct of Prior, and at their
instance Addison started the *Whig Examiner* in their
defence. Though this paper was written effectively and
with admirable temper, party polemics were little to the
taste of its author, and, after five numbers, it ceased to
exist on the 8th of October. Swift, now eager for the
triumph of the Tories, expresses his delight to Stella
by informing her, in the words of a Tory song, that "it
was down among the dead men." He himself wrote the
first of his *Examiners* on the 2d of the following Novem-

ber, and the crushing blows with which he followed it
up did much to hasten the downfall of the Ministry.
As was natural, Addison was somewhat displeased at
his friend's defection. In December Swift writes to
Stella:—"Mr. Addison and I are as different as black
and white, and I believe our friendship will go off by
this d—— business of party. He cannot bear seeing
me fall in so with the Ministry; but I love him still as
much as ever, though we seldom meet." In January
1710-11, he says: "I called at the coffee-house, where
I had not been in a week, and talked coldly awhile with
Mr. Addison ; all our friendship and dearness are off;
we are civil acquaintance, talk words of course, of when
we shall meet, and that's all. Is it not odd ?" Many
similar entries follow; but on June 26, 1711, the
record is :—"Mr. Addison and I talked as usual, and as
if we had seen one another yesterday." And on
September 14, he observes :— "This evening I met
Addison and pastoral Philips in the Park, and supped
with them in Addison's lodgings. We were very good
company, and I yet know no man half so agreeable to me
as he is. I sat with them till twelve."

It was perhaps through the influence of Swift, who
spoke warmly with the Tory Ministry on behalf of
Addison, that the latter, on the downfall of the Whigs
in the autumn of 1710, was for some time suffered to
retain the Keepership of the Records in Bermingham's
Tower, an Irish place which had been bestowed upon him
by the Queen as a special mark of the esteem with which
she regarded him, and which appears to have been worth
£400 a year.[1] In other respects his fortunes were greatly

[1] Fourth Drapier's Letter.

altered by the change of Ministry. "I have within
this twelvemonth," he writes to Wortley on the 21st of
July 1711, "lost a place of £2000 per ann., an estate
in the Indies worth £14,000, and, what is worse than all
the rest, my mistress.[1] Hear this and wonder at my
philosophy ! I find they are going to take away my
Irish place from me too ; to which I must add that I
have just resigned my fellowship, and that stocks sink
every day." In spite of these losses his circumstances
were materially different from those in which he found
himself after the fall of the previous Whig Ministry in
1702. Before the close of the year 1711 he was able
to buy the estate of Bilton, near Rugby, for £10,000.
Part of the purchase money was probably provided from
what he had saved while he was Irish Secretary and
had invested in the funds ; and part was, no doubt, made
up from the profits of the *Tatler* and the *Spectator*. Miss
Aikin says that a portion was advanced by his brother
Gulston ; but this seems to be an error. Two years
before, the Governor of Fort St. George, had died,
leaving him his executor and residuary legatee. This
is no doubt "the estate in the Indies" to which he
refers in his letter to Wortley, but he had as yet derived
no benefit from it. His brother had left his affairs in
great confusion ; the trustees were careless or dishonest ;
and though about £600 was remitted to him in the
shape of diamonds in 1713, the liquidation was not
complete till 1716, when only a small moiety of the
sum bequeathed to him came into his hands.[2]

[1] Who the "mistress" was cannot be certainly ascertained.
See, however, p. 154.
[2] Egerton MSS., British Museum (1972).

CHAPTER V.

THE *TATLER* AND *SPECTATOR*.

THE career of Addison, as described in the preceding chapters, has exemplified the great change effected in the position of men of letters in England by the Restoration and the Revolution; it is now time to exhibit him in his most characteristic light, and to show the remarkable service the eighteenth century essayists performed for English society in creating an organised public opinion. It is difficult for ourselves, who look on the action of the periodical press as part of the regular machinery of life, to appreciate the magnitude of the task accomplished by Addison and Steele in the pages of the *Tatler* and *Spectator*. Every day, week, month, and quarter, now sees the issue of a vast number of journals and magazines intended to form the opinion of every order and section of society. But in the reign of Queen Anne the only centres of society that existed were the Court, with the aristocracy that revolved about it, and the clubs and coffee-houses, in which the commercial and professional classes met to discuss matters of general interest. The *Tatler* and *Spectator* were the first organs in which an attempt was made to give form and consistency to the opinion arising out of this social

contact. But we should form a very erroneous idea of
the character of these publications if we regarded them
as the sudden productions of individual genius, written in
satisfaction of a mere temporary taste. Like all master-
pieces in art and literature, they mark the final stage of a
long and painful journey, and the merit of their inventors
consists largely in the judgment with which they profited
by the experience of many predecessors.

The first newspaper published in Europe was the
Gazzetta of Venice, which was written in manuscript,
and read aloud at certain places in the city to supply
information to the people during the war with the Turks
in 1536. In England it was not till the reign of
Elizabeth that the increased facilities of communication
and the growth of wealth caused the purveyance of
news to become a profitable employment. Towards the
end of the sixteenth century newsmongers began to
issue little pamphlets reporting extraordinary intelligence, but not issued at regular periods. The titles of
these publications, which are all of them that survive,
show that the arts with which the framers of the
placards of our own newspapers endeavour to attract
attention are of venerable antiquity : " Wonderful and
Strange newes out of Suffolke and Essex, where it
rained wheat the space of six or seven miles," 1583 ;
" Lamentable newes out of Monmouthshire, containinge
the wonderfull and fearfull accounts of the great over-
flowing of the waters in the said countrye," 1607.[1]

In 1622 one Nathaniel Butter began to publish a
newspaper bearing a fixed title and appearing at stated
intervals. It was called the *Weekly Newes from Italy and*

[1] Andrews' *History of British Journalism.*

Germanie, etc.; and was said to be printed for *Mercurius Britannicus.* This novelty provided much food for merriment to the poets, and Ben Jonson in his *Staple of News* satirises Butter, under the name of Nathaniel, in a passage which the curious reader will do well to consult, as it shows the low estimation in which newspapers were then held.[1]

Though it might appear from Jonson's dialogue that the newspapers of that day contained many items of domestic intelligence, such was scarcely the case. Butter and his contemporaries, as was natural to men who confined themselves to the publication of news without attempting to form opinion, obtained their materials almost entirely from abroad, whereby they at once aroused more vividly the imagination of their readers, and doubtless gave more scope to their own invention. Besides they were not at liberty to retail home news of that political kind which would have been of the greatest interest to the public. For a long time the evanescent character of the newspaper allowed it to escape the attention of the licenser, but the growing demand for this sort of reading at last brought it under supervision, and so strict was the control exercised over even the reports of foreign intelligence that its weekly appearance was frequently interrupted.

In 1641, however, the Star-chamber was abolished, and the heated political atmosphere of the times generated a new species of journal, in which we find the first attempt to influence opinion through the periodical press. This was the newspaper known under the generic title of *Mercury.* Many weekly publications of

---

[1] *Staple of News,* Act I. Scene 2.

this name appeared during the Civil Wars on the side of both King and Parliament, *Mercurius Anlicus* being the representative organ of the Royalist cause, and *Mercurius Pragmaticus* and *Mercurius Politicus* of the Republicans. Party animosities were thus kept alive, and proved so inconvenient to the Government that the Parliament interfered to curtail the liberty of the press. In 1647 an ordinance passed the House of Lords prohibiting any person from "making, writing, printing, selling, publishing, or uttering, or causing to be made, any book, sheet, or sheets of news whatsoever, except the same be licensed by both or either House of Parliament, with the name of the author, printer, and licenser affixed." In spite of this prohibition, which was renewed by Act of Parliament in 1662, many unlicensed periodicals continued to appear, till in 1663 the Government, finding their repressive measures insufficient, resolved to grapple with the difficulty by monopolising the right to publish news.

The author of this new project was the well-known Roger L'Estrange, who in 1663 obtained a patent assigning to him "all the sole privilege of writing, printing, and publishing all Narratives, Advertisements, Mercuries, Intelligencers, Diurnals, and other books of public intelligence." L'Estrange's journal was called the *Public Intelligencer;* it was published once a week, and in its form was a rude anticipation of the modern newspaper, containing as it did an obituary, reports of the proceedings in Parliament and in the Court of Claims, a list of the circuits of the judges, of sheriffs, Lent preachers, etc. After being continued for two years it gave place first, in 1665, to the *Oxford*

Gazette, published at Oxford, whither the Court had retired during the plague; and in 1666 to the *London Gazette*, which was under the immediate control of an Under-Secretary of State. The office of Gazetteer became henceforth a regular ministerial appointment, and was viewed with different eyes according as men were affected towards the Government. Steele, who held it, says of it: "My next appearance as a writer was in the quality of the lowest Minister of State— to wit, in the office of Gazetteer; where I worked faithfully according to order, without ever erring against the rule observed by all Ministers, to keep that paper very innocent and very insipid." Pope, on the other hand, who regarded it as an organ published to influence opinion in favour of the Government, is constant in his attacks upon it, and has immortalised it in the memorable lines in the *Dunciad* beginning: "Next plunged a feeble but a desperate pack," etc.

In 1679 the Licensing Act passed in 1662 expired, and the Parliament declined to renew it. The Court was thus left without protection against the expression of public opinion, which was daily becoming more bold and outspoken. In his extremity the King fell back on the servility of the judges, and, having procured from them an opinion that the publishing of any printed matter without license was contrary to the common law, he issued his famous Proclamation in 1680 "to prohibit and forbid all persons whatsoever to print or publish any news, book, or pamphlets of news, not licensed by his Majesty's authority."

Disregard of the proclamation was treated as a breach of the peace, and many persons were punished accordingly.   This severity produced the effect intended.   The voice of the periodical press was stifled, and the *London Gazette* was left almost in exclusive possession of the field of news.   When Monmouth landed in 1685 the King managed to obtain from Parliament a renewal of the Licensing Act for seven years, and even after the Revolution of 1688 several attempts were made by the Ministerial Whigs to prolong or to renew the operation of the Act.   In spite, however, of the violence of the organs of "Grub Street," which had grown up under it, these attempts were unsuccessful; it was justly felt that it was wiser to leave falsehood and scurrility to be gradually corrected by public opinion as speaking through an unfettered press, than to attack them by a law which they had proved themselves able to defy.   From 1682 the freedom of the press may therefore be said to date, and the lapse of the Licensing Act was the signal for a remarkable outburst of journalistic enterprise and invention.   Not only did the newspapers devoted to the report of foreign intelligence reappear in greatly increased numbers, but, whereas the old *Mercuries* had never been published more than once in the same week, the new comers made their appearance twice and some-times even three times.   In 1702 was printed the first daily newspaper, *The Daily Courant.*   It could only at starting provide material to cover one side of a half sheet of paper; but the other side was very soon covered with printed matter, in which form its existence was prolonged till 1735.

The development of party government of course encouraged the controversial capacities of the journalist, and many notorious, and some famous names are now

found among the combatants in the political arena.
On the side of the Whigs the most redoubtable champions were Daniel Defoe, of the *Review*, who was twice
imprisoned and once set in the pillory for his political
writings ; John Tutchin, of the *Observator ;* and Ridpath,
of the *Flying Post*—all of whom have obtained places in
the *Dunciad*.   The old Tories appear to have been
satisfied during the early part of Queen Anne's reign
with prosecuting the newspapers that attacked them ;
but Harley, who understood the power of the press,
engaged Prior to harass the Whigs in the *Examiner*, and
was afterwards dexterous enough to secure the invaluable
assistance of Swift for the same paper.   In opposition to
the *Examiner* in its early days the Whigs, as has been
said, started the *Whig Examiner*, under the auspices of
Addison, so that the two great historical parties had
their cases stated by the two greatest prose-writers of
the first half of the eighteenth century.

Beside the Quidnunc and the party politician, another
class of reader now appeared demanding aliment in the
press.   Men of active and curious minds, with a little
leisure and a large love of discussion, loungers at Will's
or at the Grecian Coffee-Houses, were anxious to have
their doubts on all subjects resolved by a printed oracle.
Their tastes were gratified by the ingenuity of John
Dunton, whose strange account of his *Life and Errors*
throws a strong light on the literary history of this
period.   In 1690 Dunton published his *Athenian Gazette*,
the name of which he afterwards altered to the *Athenian
Mercury*.   The object of this paper was to answer
questions put to the editor by the public.   These were
of all kinds on religion, casuistry, love, literature, and

manners, no question being too subtle or absurd to
extract a reply from the conductor of the paper. The
Athenian Mercury seems to have been read by as many
distinguished men of the period as *Notes and Queries* in
our own time, and there can be no doubt that the quaint
humours it originated gave the first hint to the inventors
of the *Tatler* and the *Spectator*.

Advertisements were inserted in the newspapers at
a comparatively early period of their existence. The
editor acted as middleman between the advertiser and
the public, and made his announcements in a style of
easy frankness which will appear to the modern reader
extremely refreshing. Thus in the "Collection for the
Improvement of Husbandry and Trade" (1682) there are
the following :—

"If I can meet with a sober man that has a counter-
tenor voice, I can help him to a place worth thirty pound
the year or more.

"If any noble or other gentleman wants a porter that is
very lusty, comely, and six foot high and two inches, I can
help.

"I want a complete young man that will wear a livery,
to wait on a very valuable gentleman; but he must know
how to play on a violin or flute.

"I want a genteel footman that can play on the violin,
to wait on a person of honour." [1]

Everything was now prepared for the production of
a class of newspaper designed to form and direct public
opinion on rational principles. The press was emancipated from State control; a reading public had constituted itself out of the *habitues* of the coffee-houses and
clubs; nothing was wanted but an inventive genius to
adapt the materials at his disposal to the circumstances

[1] Andrews' *History of British Journalism.*

of the time.   The required hero was not long in making his appearance.

Richard Steele, the son of an official under the Irish Government, was, above all things, "a creature of ebullient heart." Impulse and sentiment were with him always far stronger motives of action than reason, principle, or even interest. He left Oxford, without taking a degree, from an ardent desire to serve in the army, thereby sacrificing his prospect of succeeding to a family estate ; his extravagance and dissipation while serving in the cavalry were notorious ; yet this did not dull the clearness of his moral perceptions, for it was while his excesses were at their height that he dedicated to his commanding officer, Lord Cutts, his *Christian Hero*. Vehement in his political, as in all other feelings, he did not hesitate to resign the office he held under the Tory Government in 1711 in order to attack it for what he considered its treachery to the country ; but he was equally outspoken, and with equal disadvantage to himself, when he found himself at a later period in disagreement with the Whigs.   He had great fertility of invention, strong natural humour, true though uncultivated taste, and inexhaustible human sympathy.

His varied experience had made him well acquainted with life and character, and in his office of Gazetteer he had had an opportunity of watching the eccentricities of the public taste, which, now emancipated from restraint, began vaguely to feel after new ideals.   That, under such circumstances, he should have formed the design of treating current events from a humorous point of view was only natural, but he was indebted for the form of his newspaper to the most original genius of the age.   Swift

had early in the eighteenth century exercised his ironical
vein by treating the everyday occurrences of life in a
mock - heroic style.   Among his pieces of this kind
that were most successful in catching the public taste
were the humorous predictions of the death of Partridge,
the astrologer, signed with the name of Isaac Bickerstaff.   Steele, seizing on the name and character of
Partridge's fictitious rival, turned him with much
pleasantry into the editor of a new journal, the design of which he makes Isaac describe as follows :—

" The state of conversation and business in this town
having long been perplexed with Pretenders in both kinds, in
order to open men's minds against such abuses, it appeared
no unprofitable undertaking to publish a Paper, which should
observe upon the manners of the pleasurable, as well as the
busy part of mankind.   To make this generally read, it
seemed the most proper method to form it by way of a Letter
of Intelligence, consisting of such parts as might gratify the
curiosity of persons of all conditions and of each sex. . . .
The general purposes of this Paper is to expose the false
arts of life, to pull off the disguises of cunning, vanity, and
affectation, and to recommend a general simplicity in our
dress, our discourse, and our behaviour." [1]

The name of the *Tatler*, Isaac informs us, was "invented
in honour of the fair sex," for whose entertainment the
new paper was largely designed.   It appeared three times
a week, and its price was a penny, though it seems that
the first number, published April 12, 1709, was distributed
gratis as an advertisement.   In order to make the contents of the paper varied it was divided into five portions,
of which the editor gives the following account :—

" All accounts of Gallantry, Pleasure, and Entertainment,
shall be under the article of White's Chocolate-House ; Poetry

---

[1] *Tatler*, No. 1.

under that of Will's Coffee-House ; Learning under the title
of Grecian ; Foreign and Domestic News you will have from
Saint James' Coffee-House ; and what else I have to offer on
any other subject shall be dated from my own apartment." [1]

In this division we see the importance of the coffee-
houses as the natural centres of intelligence and opinion.
Of the four houses mentioned, St. James's and White's,
both of them in St. James's Street, were the chief haunts
of statesmen and men of fashion, and the latter had
acquired an infamous notoriety for the ruinous gambling
of its *habitues*.   Will's in Russell Street, Covent Garden,
kept up the reputation which it had procured in Dryden's
time as the favourite meeting-place of men of letters ;
while the Grecian in Devereux Court in the Strand, which
was the oldest coffee-house in London, afforded a convenient *rendezvous* for the learned Templars.   At starting
the design announced in the first number was adhered
to with tolerable fidelity.   The paper dated from St.
James' Coffee-House was always devoted to the recital
of foreign news ; that from Will's either criticised the
current dramas, or contained a copy of verses from some
author of repute, or a piece of general literary criticism ;
the latest gossip at White's was reproduced in a fictitious
form and with added colour.   Advertisements were also
inserted ; and half a sheet of the paper was left blank,
in order that at the last moment the most recent intelligence might be added in manuscript after the manner of
the contemporary news-letters.   In all these respects
the character of the newspaper was preserved ; but in
the method of treating news adopted by the editor there
was a constant tendency to subordinate matter of fact
to the elements of humour, fiction, and sentiment.   In

[1] *Tatler*, No. 1.

his survey of the manners of the time Isaac, as an
astrologer, was assisted by a familiar spirit, named
Pacolet, who revealed to him the motives and secrets
of men; his sister, Mrs. Jenny Distaff, was occasionally
deputed to produce the paper from the wizard's "own
apartment;" and Kidney, the waiter at St. James'
Coffee-House, was humorously represented as the chief
authority in all matters of foreign intelligence.

The mottoes assumed by the *Tatler* at different periods
of its existence mark the stages of its development. On
its first appearance, when Steele seems to have intended
it to be little more than a lively record of news, the
motto placed at the head of each paper was—

> " Quidquid agunt homines,
>   nostri est farrago libelli."

It soon became evident, however, that its true function
was not merely to report the actions of men, but to
discuss the propriety of their actions; and by the time
that sufficient material had accumulated to constitute a
volume, the essayists felt themselves justified in appro-
priating the words used by Pliny in the preface to his
Natural History:—

> " Nemo apud nos qui idem tentaverit : equidem sentio
> peculiarem in studiis causam eorum esse, qui difficultatibus
> victis, utilitatem juvandi, protulerunt gratiæ placendi.   Res
> ardua vetustis novitatem dare, novis auctoritatem, obsoletis
> nitorem, fastidits gratiam, dubiis fidem, omnibus vero
> naturam, et naturæ suæ omnia.   Itaque NON ASSECUTIS
> *voluisse,* abunde pulchrum atque magnificum est."

The disguise of the mock astrologer proved very useful to Steele in his character of moralist.   It enabled
him to give free utterance to his better feelings without the risk of incurring the charge of inconsistency or

hypocrisy, and nothing can be more honourable to him than the open manner in which he acknowledges his own unfitness for the position of a moralist : " I shall not carry my humility so far," says he, " as to call myself a vicious man, but at the same time must confess my life is at best but pardonable.   With no greater character than this, a man would make but an indifferent progress in attacking prevailing and fashionable vices, which Mr. Bickerstaff has done with a freedom of spirit that would have lost both its beauty and efficacy had it been pretended to by Mr. Steele." [1]

As Steele cannot claim the sole merit of having invented the form of the *Tatler* so too it must be remembered that he could never have addressed society in the high moral tone assumed by Bickerstaff if the road had not been prepared for him by others. One name among his predecessors stands out with a special title to honourable record.   Since the Restoration the chief school of manners had been the stage, and the flagrant example of immorality set by the Court had been bettered by the invention of the comic dramatists of the period.   Indecency was the fashion ; religion and sobriety were identified by the polite world with Puritanism and hypocrisy.   Even the Church had not yet ventured to say a word in behalf of virtue against the prevailing taste, and when at last a clergyman raised his voice on behalf of the principles which he professed, the blow which he dealt to his antagonists was the more damaging because it was entirely unexpected.   Jeremy Collier was not only a Tory but a Jacobite, not only a High Churchman but a Nonjuror,

[1] *Tatler*, No. 271.

who had been outlawed for his fidelity to the principles
of Legitimism ; and that such a man should have published the *Short View of the Immorality and Profaneness of
the English Stage*, reflecting, as the book did, in the
strongest manner on the manners of the fallen dynasty,
was as astounding as thunder from a clear sky. Collier,
however, was a man of sincere piety, whose mind was
for the moment occupied only by the overwhelming
danger of the evil which he proposed to attack. It is
true that his method of attack was cumbrous, and that
his conclusions were far too sweeping and often unjust;
nevertheless the general truth of his criticisms was felt
to be irresistible. Congreve and Vanbrugh each attempted
an apology for their profession ; both, however, showed
their perception of the weakness of their position by
correcting or recasting scenes in their comedies to which
Collier had objected.   Dryden accepted the reproof in a
nobler spirit.   Even while he had pandered to the taste
of the times he had been conscious of his treachery to
the cause of true art, and had broken out in a fine
passage in his *Ode to the Memory of Mrs. Killigrew :*—

> " O gracious God ! how far have we
>   Profaned thy heavenly gift of poesy !
>   Made prostitute and profligate the Muse,
>   Debased to each obscene and impious use !

> " O wretched we ! why were we hurried down
>   This lubrique and adulterous age
>   (Nay, added fat pollutions of our own)
>   To increase the streaming ordure of the stage ?"

When Collier attacked him he bent his head in sub-
mission.   "In many things," says he, "he has taxed me
justly, and I have pleaded guilty to all thought and ex-

pressions of mine which can be truly argued of obscenity, profaneness, or immorality, and retract them. If he be my enemy, let him triumph; if he be my friend, as I have given him no personal occasion to be otherwise, he will be glad of my repentance." [1]

The first blow against fashionable immorality having been boldly struck, was followed up systematically. In 1690 was founded " The Society for the Reformation of Manners," which published every year an account of the progress made in suppressing profaneness and debauchery by its means. It continued its operations till 1738, and during its existence prosecuted, according to its own calculations, 101,683 persons. William III. showed himself prompt to encourage the movement which his subjects had begun. The *London Gazette* of 27th February 1698-9 contains a report of the following remarkable order :—

" His Majesty being informed, That, notwithstanding an order made the 4th of June 1697 by the Earl of Sunderland, then Lord Chamberlain of His Majesty's Household, to prevent the Prophaneness and Immorality of the Stage; several Plays have been lately acted containing expressions contrary to Religion and Good Manners : and whereas the Master of the Revels has represented, That, in contempt of the said order, the actors do often neglect to leave out such Prophane and Indecent expressions as he has thought proper to be omitted. These are therefore to signifie his Majesty's pleasure, that you do not hereafter presume to act anything in any play contrary to Religion and Good Manners as you shall answer it at your utmost peril. Given under my Hand this 18th of February 1698. In the eleventh year of his Majesty's reign."

It is difficult to realise in reading the terms of this order that only thirteen years had elapsed since the

[1] *Preface to the Fables.*

death of Charles II., and undoubtedly a very large share
of the credit due for such a revolution in the public
taste is to be assigned to Collier. Collier, however,
did nothing in a literary or artistic sense to improve the
character of English literature. His severity, uncom-
promising as that of the Puritans, inspired Vice with
terror, but could not plead with persuasion on behalf of
Virtue ; his sweeping conclusions struck at the roots of
Art as well as of Immorality. He sought to destroy the
drama and kindred pleasures of the Imagination, not to
reform them. What the age needed was a writer to
satisfy its natural desires for healthy and rational
amusement, and Steele with his strongly-developed two-
fold character was the man of all others to bridge over
the chasm between irreligious licentiousness and Puri-
tanical rigidity. Driven headlong on one side of his
nature towards all the tastes and pleasures which
absorbed the Court of Charles II., his heart in the midst
of his dissipation never ceased to approve of whatever
was great, noble, and generous. He has described himself with much feeling in his disquisition on the *Rake*, a
character which he says many men are desirous of
assuming without any natural qualifications for supporting it :—

"A Rake," says he, "is a man always to be pitied ; and
if he lives one day is certainly reclaimed ; for his faults proceed not from choice or inclination, but from strong passions
and appetites, which are in youth too violent for the curb of
reason, good sense, good manners, and good nature ; all
which he must have by nature and education before he can
be allowed to be or to have been of this order. . . . His
desires run away with him through the strength and force
of a lively imagination, which hurries him on to unlawful
pleasures before reason has power to come in to his rescue."

That impulsiveness of feeling which is here described,
and which was the cause of so many of Steele's failings
in real life, made him the most powerful and persuasive
advocate of Virtue in fiction. Of all the imaginative
English essayists he is the most truly natural. His
large heart seems to rush out in sympathy with any tale
of sorrow or exhibition of magnanimity; and, even in
criticism, his true natural instinct, joined to his consti-
tutional enthusiasm often raises his judgments to a level
with those of Addison himself, as in his excellent essay
in the *Spectator* on Raphael's cartoons.   Examples of
these characteristics in his style are to be found in the
Story of Unnion and Valentine,[1] and in the fine paper
describing two tragedies of real life;[2] in the series of
papers on duelling, occasioned by a duel into which he
was himself forced against his own inclination;[3] and in
the sound advice which Isaac gives to his half-sister
Jenny on the morrow of her marriage.[4]   Perhaps, however, the chivalry and generosity of feeling which make
Steele's writings so attractive are most apparent in the
delightful paper containing the letter of Serjeant Hall
from the camp before Mons.   After pointing out to his
readers the admirable features in the serjeant's simple
letter, Steele concludes as follows :—

" If we consider the heap of an army, utterly out of all
prospect of rising and preferment, as they certainly are, and
such great things executed by them, it is hard to account for
the motive of their gallantry.   But to me, who was a cadet
at the battle of Coldstream in Scotland when Monk charged
at the head of the regiment now called Coldstream, from the
victory of that day—I remember it as well as if it were yes-

---

[1] *Tatler*, No. 5.   [2] *Ib.*, No. 82.
[3] *Ib.*, Nos. 25, 26, 28, 29, 38, 39.   [4] *Ib.*, No. 85.

terday, I stood on the left of old West, who I believe is now
at Chelsea — I say to me, who know very well this part of
mankind, I take the gallantry of private soldiers to proceed
from the same, if not from a nobler, impulse than that of
gentlemen and officers. They have the same taste of being
acceptable to their friends, and go through the difficulties of
that profession by the same irresistible charm of fellowship
and the communication of joys and sorrows which quickens
the relish of pleasure and abates the anguish of pain. Add
to this that they have the same regard to fame, though they
do not expect so great a share as men above them hope for;
but I will engage Serjeant Hall would die ten thousand
deaths rather than that a word should be spoken at the Red
Lettice, or any part of the Butcher Row, in prejudice to his
courage or honesty. If you will have my opinion, then, of
the Serjeant's letter, I pronounce the style to be mixed, but
truly epistolary; the sentiment relating to his own wound
in the sublime; the postscript of Pegg Hartwell in the gay;
and the whole the picture of the bravest sort of men, that is
to say, a man of great courage and small hopes." [1]

With such excellences of style and sentiment it is no
wonder that the *Tatler* rapidly established itself in public
favour. It was a novel experience for the general reader
to be provided three times a week with entertainment
that pleased his imagination without offending his sense
of decency or his religious instincts. But a new hand
shortly appeared in the *Tatler*, which was destined to
carry the art of periodical essay-writing to a perfection
beside which even the humour of Steele appears rude and
unpolished. Addison and Steele had been friends since
boyhood. They had been contemporaries at the Charter
House, and, as we have seen, Steele had sometimes spent
his holidays in the parsonage of Addison's father. He
was a postmaster at Merton about the same time that his

---

[1] *Tatler*, No. 87.

friend was a Fellow of Magdalen. The admiration which he conceived for the hero of his boyhood lasted, as so often happens, through life ; he exhibited his veneration for him in all places, and even when Addison indulged his humour at his expense he showed no resentment. Addison, on his side, seems to have treated Steele with a kind of gracious condescension. The latter was one of the few intimate friends to whom he unbent in conversation ; and while he was Under-Secretary of State he aided him in the production of *The Tender Husband*, which was dedicated to him by the author. Of this play Steele afterwards declared with characteristic impulse that many of the most admired passages were the work of his friend, and that he "thought very meanly of himself that he had never publicly avowed it."

The authorship of the *Tatler* was at first kept secret to all the world. It is said that the hand of Steele discovered itself to Addison on reading in the fifth number a remark which he remembered to have himself made to Steele on the judgment of Virgil as shown in the appellation of "Dux Trojanus," which the Latin poet assigns to Æneas, when describing his adventure with Dido in the cave, in the place of the usual epithet of "pius " or "pater." Thereupon he offered his services as a contributor, and these were of course gladly accepted. The first paper sent by Addison to the *Tatler* was No. 18, wherein is displayed that inimitable art which makes a man appear infinitely ridiculous by the ironical commendation of his offences against right reason and good taste. The subject is the approaching peace with France, and it is noticeable that the article of foreign news, which had been treated in previous

Tatlers with complete seriousness, is here for the first
time invested with an air of pleasantry.   The distress of
the news-writers at the prospect of peace is thus described :—

"There is another sort of gentlemen whom I am much
more concerned for, and that is the ingenious fraternity of
which I have the honour to be an unworthy member; I
mean the news-writers of Great Britain, whether Post-men or
Post-boys, or by what other name or title soever dignified
or distinguished.   The case of these gentlemen is, I think,
more hard than that of the soldiers, considering that they
have taken more towns and fought more battles.   They have
been upon parties and skirmishes when our armies have lain
still, and given the general assault to many a place when the
besiegers were quiet in their trenches.   They have made us
masters of several strong towns many weeks before our gene-
rals could do it, and completed victories when our greatest
captains have been glad to come off with a drawn battle.
Where Prince Eugene has slain his thousands Boyer has slain
his ten thousands.   This gentleman can indeed be never
enough commended for his courage and intrepidity during
this whole war : he has laid about him with an inexpressible
fury, and, like offended Marius of ancient Rome, made such
havoc among his countrymen as must be the work of two or
three ages to repair. . . .   It is impossible for this ingenious
sort of men to subsist after a peace : every one remembers
the shifts they were driven to in the reign of King Charles
the Second, when they could not furnish out a single paper
of news without lighting up a comet in Germany or a fire in
Moscow.   There scarce appeared a letter without a paragraph
on an earthquake.   Prodigies were grown so familiar that
they had lost their name, as a great poet of that age has it.
I remember Mr. Dyer, who is justly looked upon by all the
foxhunters in the nation as the greatest statesman our country
has produced, was particularly famous for dealing in whales,
in so much that in five months' time (for I had the curiosity
to examine his letters on that occasion) he brought three into
the mouth of the river Thames, besides two porpusses and a
sturgeon."

The appearance of Addison as a regular contributor
to the *Tatler* gradually brought about a revolution in the
character of the paper. For some time longer, indeed,
articles continued to be dated from the different coffee-
houses, but only slight efforts were made to distinguish
the materials furnished from White's, Will's, or Isaac's
own apartment. When the hundredth number was
reached a fresh address is given at Shere Lane, where
the astrologer lived, and henceforward the papers from
White's and Will's grow extremely rare; those from the
Grecian may be said to disappear; and the foreign
intelligence, dated from St. James', whenever it is
inserted, which is seldom, is as often as not made the
text of a literary disquisition. Allegories become frequent, and the letters sent, or supposed to be sent, to
Isaac at his home address furnish the material for many
numbers. The Essay, in fact, or that part of the newspaper which goes to form public opinion, preponderates
greatly over that portion which is devoted to the report
of news. Spence quotes from a Mr. Chute: " I have
heard Sir Richard Steele say that, though he had a
greater share in the *Tatlers* than in the *Spectators*, he
thought the news article in the first of these was what
contributed much to their success."[1]   Chute, however,
seems to speak with a certain grudge against Addison,
and the statement ascribed by him to Steele is in-
trinsically improbable. It is not very likely that, as the
proprietor of the *Tatler*, he would have dispensed with
any element in it that contributed to its popularity, yet
after No. 100 the news articles are seldom found. The
truth is that Steele recognised the superiority of Addi-

[1] Spence's *Anecdotes*, p. 325.

son's style, and, with his usual quickness, accommodated
the form of his journal to the genius of the new contributor.

"I have only one gentleman," says he in the preface to
the *Tatler*, "who will be nameless, to thank for any frequent
assistance to me, which indeed it would have been barbarous
in him to have denied to one with whom he has lived in
intimacy from childhood, considering the great ease with
which he is able to despatch the most entertaining pieces of
this nature. This good office he performed with such force
of genius, humour, wit, and learning, that I fared like a dis-
tressed prince who calls in a powerful neighbour to his aid ;
I was undone by my own auxiliary ; when I had once called
him in I could not subsist without dependence on him."

With his usual enthusiastic generosity Steele in this
passage unduly depreciates his own merits to exalt the
genius of his friend. A comparison of the amount of
material furnished to the *Tatler* by Addison and Steele
respectively shows that out of 271 numbers the latter
contributed 188 and the former only 42. Nor is the
disparity in quantity entirely balanced by the superior
quality of Addison's papers. Though it was, doubtless,
his fine workmanship and admirable method which
carried to perfection the style of writing initiated in the
Tatler, yet there is scarcely a department of essay-
writing developed in the *Spectator* which does not trace
its origin to Steele. It is Steele who first ventures to
raise his voice against the prevailing dramatic taste of
the age on behalf of the superior morality and art of
Shakespeare's plays.

"Of all men living," says he in the eighth *Tatler*, "I pity
players (who must be men of good understanding to be
capable of being such) that they are obliged to repeat and

assume proper gestures for representing things of which their reason must be ashamed, and which they must disdain their audience for approving. The amendment of these low gratifications is only to be made by people of condition, by encouraging the noble representation of the noble characters drawn by Shakespeare and others, from whence it is impossible to return without strong impressions of honour and humanity. On these occasions distress is laid before us with all its causes and consequences, and our resentment placed according to the merit of the person afflicted. Were dramas of this nature more acceptable to the taste of the town, men who have genius would bend their studies to excel in them."

Steele, too, it was who attacked with all the vigour of which he was capable the fashionable vice of gambling. So severe were his comments on this subject in the *Tatler* that he raised against himself the fierce resentment of the whole community of sharpers, though he was fortunate enough at the same time to enlist the sympathies of the better part of society. "Lord Forbes," says Mr. Nichols, the antiquary, in his notes to the *Tatler*, "happened to be in company with the two military gentlemen just mentioned" (Major-General Davenport and Brigadier Bisset) "in St. James' Coffee-House when two or three well-dressed men, all unknown to his lordship or his company, came into the room, and in a public outrageous manner abused Captain Steele as the author of the *Tatler*. One of them, with great audacity and vehemence, swore that he would cut Steele's throat or teach him better manners. 'In this country,' said Lord Forbes, 'you will find it easier to cut a purse than to cut a throat.' His brother officers instantly joined with his lordship, and turned the cut-throats out of the coffee-house with every mark of disgrace." [1]

[1] *Tatler*, vol. iv. p. 545 (Nichol's edition).

The practice of duelling also, which had hitherto passed unreproved, was censured by Steele in a series of papers in the *Tatler*, which seemed to have been written on an occasion when, having been forced to fight much against his will, he had the misfortune dangerously to wound his antagonist.[1] The sketches of character studied from life, and the letters from fictitious correspondents, both of which form so noticeable a feature in the *Spectator*, appear roughly, but yet distinctly, drafted in the *Tatler*. Even the papers of literary criticism, afterwards so fully elaborated by Addison, are anticipated by his friend, who may fairly claim the honour to have been the first to speak with adequate respect of the genius of Milton.[2] In a word, whatever was perfected by Addison was begun by Steele ; if the one has for ever associated his name with the *Spectator*, the other may justly appropriate the credit of the *Tatler*, a work which bears to its successor the same kind of relation that the frescoes of Masaccio bear, in point of dramatic feeling and style, to those of Raphael ; the later productions deserving honour for finish of execution, the earlier for priority of invention.

The *Tatler* was published till the 2d of January 1710-11, and was discontinued, according to Steele's own account, because the public had penetrated his disguise, and he was therefore no longer able to preach with effect in the person of Bickerstaff. It may be doubted whether this was his real motive for abandoning the paper. He had been long known as its conductor, and that his readers had shown no disinclination to listen to him is proved not only by the large circulation of each number

---

[1] See p. 97, note 3.   [2] *Tatler*, No. 6.

of the *Tatler*, but by the extensive sale of the successive
volumes of the collected papers at the high price of a
guinea apiece.   He was, in all probability, led to drop the
publication by finding that the political element that
the paper contained was a source of embarrassment
to him.   His sympathies were vehemently Whig ; the
Tatler from the beginning had celebrated the virtues of
Marlborough and his friends, both directly and under
cover of fiction ; and he had been rewarded for his services with a commissionership of the Stamp-office.   When
the Whig Ministry fell in 1710, Harley, setting a just
value on the abilities of Steele, left him in the enjoy-
ment of his office and expressed his desire to serve him
in any other way.   Under these circumstances, Steele no
doubt felt it incumbent on him to discontinue a paper
which, both from its design and its traditions, would have
tempted him into the expression of his political partialities.

For two months therefore "the censorship of Great
Britain," as he himself expressed it, "remained in commission," until Addison and he once more returned to
discharge the duties of the office in the *Spectator*, the
first number of which was published on the 1st of March
1710-11.   The *Tatler* had only been issued three times a
week, but the conductors of the new paper were now so
confident in their own resources and in the favour of the
public that they undertook to bring out one number
daily.   The new paper at once exhibited the impress of
Addison's genius, which had gradually transformed the
character of the *Tatler* itself.   The latter was originally,
in every sense of the word, a newspaper, but the *Spectator*
from the first indulged his humour at the expense of the
clubs of Quidnuncs.

"There is," says he, "another set of men that I must likewise lay a claim to as being altogether unfurnished with ideas till the business and conversation of the day has supplied them. I have often considered these poor souls with an eye of great commiseration when I have heard them asking the first man they have met with whether there was any news stirring, and by that means gathering together materials for thinking. These needy persons do not know what to talk of till about twelve o'clock in the morning; for by that time they are pretty good judges of the weather, know which way the wind sets, and whether the Dutch mail be come in. As they lie at the mercy of the first man they meet, and are grave or impertinent all the day long, according to the notions which they have imbibed in the morning, I would earnestly entreat them not to stir out of their chambers till they have read this paper; and do promise them that I will daily instil into them such sound and wholesome sentiments as shall have a good effect on their conversation for the ensuing twelve hours." [1]

For these, and other men of leisure, a kind of paper differing from the *Tatler*, which proposed only to retail the various species of gossip in the coffee-houses, was required, and the new entertainment was provided by the original design of an imaginary club, consisting of several ideal types of character grouped round the central figure of the Spectator. They represent considerable classes or sections of the community, and are, as a rule, men of strongly marked opinions, prejudices, and foibles, which furnish inexhaustible matter of comment to the Spectator himself, who delivers the judgments of reason and common-sense. Sir Roger de Coverley, with his simplicity, his high sense of honour, and his old-world reminiscences, reflects the country gentleman of the best kind; Sir Andrew Freeport expresses the opinions of

[1] *Spectator*, No. 10.

the enterprising, hard-headed, and rather hard-hearted
monied interest; Captain Sentry speaks for the army;
the Templar for the world of taste and learning; the
clergyman for theology and philosophy; while Will
Honeycomb, the elderly man of fashion, gives the
Spectator many opportunities for criticising the traditions
of morality and breeding surviving from the days of the
Restoration.   Thus, instead of the division of places
which determined the arrangement of the *Tatler*, the
different subjects treated in the *Spectator* are distributed
among a variety of persons : the Templar is substituted
for the Grecian Coffee-House and Will's; Will Honeycomb takes the place of White's; and Captain Sentry,
whose appearances are rare, stands for the more voluminous article on foreign intelligence published in the old
periodical under the head of St. James's.   The Spectator
himself finds a natural prototype in Isaac Bickerstaff,
but his character is drawn with a far greater finish and
delicacy, and is much more essential to the design of the
paper which he conducts, than was that of the old
astrologer.

The aim of the *Spectator* was to establish a rational
standard of conduct in morals, manners, art, and literature.

"Since," says he in one of his early numbers, "I have
raised to myself so great an audience, I shall spare no pains
to make their instruction agreeable and their diversion useful.
For which reason I shall endeavour to enliven morality with
wit, and to temper wit with morality, that my readers may,
if possible, both ways find their account in the speculation of
the day.   And to the end that their virtue and discretion
may not be short, transient, intermitting starts of thought, I
have resolved to refresh their memories from day to day till

I have recovered them out of that desperate state of vice and folly into which the age has fallen. The mind that lies fallow but a single day sprouts up in follies that are only to be killed by a constant and assiduous culture. It was said of Socrates that he brought philosophy down from heaven to inhabit among men ; and I shall be ambitious to have it said of me that I have brought philosophy out of closets and libraries, schools and colleges, to dwell in clubs and assemblies, at tea-tables and in coffee-houses." [1]

Johnson, in his *Life of Addison*, says that the task undertaken in the *Spectator* was " first attempted by Casa in his book of *Manners*, and Castiglione in his *Courtier ;* two books yet celebrated in Italy for purity and elegance, and which, if they are now less read, are neglected only because they have effected that reformation which their authors intended and their precepts now are no longer wanted." He afterwards praises the *Tatler* and *Spectator* by saying that they "adjusted, like Casa, the unsettled practice of daily intercourse by propriety and politeness ; and, like La Bruyère, exhibited the characters and manners of the age." This commendation scarcely does justice to the work of Addison and Steele. Casa, a man equally distinguished for profligacy and politeness, merely codified in his *Galateo* the laws of good manners which prevailed in his age. He is the Lord Chesterfield of Italy. Castiglione gives instructions to the young courtier how to behave in such a manner as to make himself agreeable to his prince. La Bruyère's characters are no doubt the literary models of those which appear in the *Spectator*. But La Bruyère merely described what he saw, with admirable wit, urbanity, and scholarship, but without

[1] *Spectator*, No. 10.

any of the earnestness of a moral reformer. He could
never have conceived the character of Sir Roger de
Coverley; and, though he was ready enough to satirise
the follies of society as an observer from the outside, to
bring "philosophy out of closets and libraries, to dwell
in clubs and assemblies," was far from being his ambition.
He would probably have thought the publication of a
newspaper scarcely consistent with his position as a
gentleman.

A very large portion of the *Spectator* is devoted to
reflections on the manners of women. Addison saw
clearly how important a part the female sex was destined
to play in the formation of English taste and manners.
Removed from the pedestal of enthusiastic devotion on
which they had been placed during the feudal ages,
women were treated under the Restoration as mere play-
things and luxuries. As manners became more decent
they found themselves secured in their emancipated
position, but destitute of serious and rational employment.
It was Addison's object, therefore, to enlist the aid of
female genius in softening, refining, and moderating the
gross and conflicting tastes of a half-civilised society.

"There are none," he says, "to whom this paper will be
more useful than to the female world. I have often thought
there has not been sufficient pains taken in finding out proper
employments and diversions for the fair ones. Their amuse-
ments seem contrived for them, rather as they are women,
than as they are reasonable creatures ; and are more adapted
to the sex than to the species. The toilet is their great scene
of business, and the right adjustment of their hair the principal employment of their lives. The sorting of a suit of
ribands is reckoned a very good morning's work; and if they
make an excursion to a mercer's or a toy shop, so great a
fatigue makes them unfit for anything else all the day after.

Their more serious occupations are sewing and embroidery, and their greatest drudgery the preparations of jellies and sweetmeats. This, I say, is the state of ordinary women; though I know there are multitudes of those of a more elevated life and conversation, that move in an exalted sphere of knowledge and virtue, that join all the beauties of the mind to the ornaments of dress, and inspire a kind of awe and respect, as well as of love, into their male beholders. I hope to increase the number of these by publishing this daily paper, which I shall always endeavour to make an innocent, if not an improving entertainment, and by that means, at least, divert the minds of my female readers from greater trifles." [1]

To some of the vigorous spirits of the age the mild and social character of the *Spectator's* satire did not commend itself. Swift, who had contributed several papers to the *Tatler* while it was in its infancy, found it too feminine for his taste. "I will not meddle with the *Spectator*," says he in his *Journal to Stella*, "let him *fair sex* it to the world's end." Personal pique, however, may have done as much as a differing taste to depreciate the *Spectator* in the eyes of the author of the *Tale of a Tub*, for he elsewhere acknowledges its merits. "The *Spectator*," he writes to Stella, "is written by Steele, with Addison's help; it is often very pretty . . . but I never see him (Steele) or Addison." That part of the public to whom the paper was specially addressed read it with keen relish. In the ninety-second number a correspondent signing herself "Leonora" [2] writes:—

"Mr. Spectator,—Your paper is part of my tea-equipage; and my servant knows my humour so well that, calling for my breakfast this morning (it being past my usual hour), she answered, the *Spectator* was not yet come in, but the tea-kettle boiled, and she expected it every moment."

---

[1] *Spectator*, No. 10.   [2] The writer was a Miss Shepherd.

In a subsequent number "Thomas Trusty" writes :—

"I constantly peruse your paper as I smoke my morning's pipe (though I can't forbear reading the motto before I fill and light), and really it gives a grateful relish to every whiff ; each paragraph is fraught either with useful or delightful notions, and I never fail of being highly diverted or improved. The variety of your subjects surprises me as much as a box of pictures did formerly, in which there was only one face, that by pulling some pieces of isinglass over it was changed into a grave senator or a merry-andrew, a polished lady or a nun, a beau or a blackamoor, a prude or a coquette, a country squire or a conjuror, with many other different representations very entertaining (as you are), though still the same at the bottom." [1]

The *Spectator* was read in all parts of the country.

"I must confess," says Addison as his task was drawing to an end, "that I am not a little gratified and obliged by that concern which appears in this great city upon my present design of laying down this paper. It is likewise with much satisfaction that I find some of the most outlying parts of the kingdom alarmed upon this occasion, having received letters to expostulate with me about it from several of my readers of the remotest boroughs of Great Britain." [2]

With how keen an interest the public entered into the humour of the paper is shown by the following letter, signed "Philo-Spec":—

"I was this morning in a company of your well-wishers, when we read over, with great satisfaction, Tully's observations on action adapted to the British theatre, though, by the way, we were very sorry to find that you have disposed of another member of your club. Poor Sir Roger is dead, and the worthy clergyman dying ; Captain Sentry has taken possession of a fair estate ; Will Honeycomb has married a farmer's daughter ; and the Templar withdraws himself into the business of his own profession." [3]

---

[1] *Spectator*, No. 134.   [2] *Ibid.*, No. 553.   [3] *Ibid.*, No. 542.

It is no wonder that readers anticipated with regret the dissolution of a society that had provided them with so much delicate entertainment. Admirably as the club was designed for maintaining that variety of treatment on which Mr. Trusty comments in the letter quoted above, the execution of the design is deserving of even greater admiration. The skill with which the grave speculations of the *Spectator* are contrasted with the lively observations of Will Honeycomb on the fashions of the age, and these again are diversified with papers descriptive of character or adorned with fiction, while the letters from the public outside form a running commentary on the conduct of the paper, cannot be justly appreciated without a certain effort of thought. But it may safely be said that, to have provided society day after day for more than two years with a species of entertainment which, nearly two centuries later, retains all its old power to interest and delight, is an achievement unique in the history of literature. Even apart from the exquisite art displayed in their grouping, the matter of many of the essays in the *Spectator* is still valuable. The vivid descriptions of contemporary manners; the inimitable series of sketches of Sir Roger de Coverley; the criticisms in the papers on *True and False Wit* and Milton's *Paradise Lost ;* have scarcely less significance for ourselves than for the society for which they were immediately written.

Addison's own papers were 274 in number, as against 236 contributed by Steele. They were, as a rule, signed with one of the four letters C. L. I. O., either because, as Tickell seems to hint in his *Elegy*, they composed the name of one of the Muses, or, as later scholars have conjectured, because they were respectively written from four different localities, viz. Chelsea, London, Islington, and the Office.

The sale of the *Spectator* was doubtless very large relatively to the number of readers in Queen Anne's reign. Johnson, indeed, computes the number sold daily to have been only sixteen hundred and eighty, but he seems to have overlooked what Addison himself says on the subject very shortly after the paper had been started : "My publisher tells me that there are already three thousand of them distributed every day."[1] This number must have gone on increasing with the growing reputation of the *Spectator*. When the Preface of the *Four Sermons* of Dr. Fleetwood, Bishop of Llandaff, was suppressed by order of the House of Commons, the *Spectator* printed it in its 384th number, thus conveying, as the Bishop said in a letter to Burnet, Bishop of Salisbury, "fourteen thousand copies of the condemned preface into people's hands that would otherwise have never seen or heard of it." Making allowance for the extraordinary character of the number, it is not unreasonable to conclude that the usual daily issue of the *Spectator* to readers in all parts of the kingdom would, towards the close of its career, have reached ten thousand copies. The separate papers were afterwards collected into octavo volumes, which were sold, like the volumes of the *Tatler*, for a guinea a-piece. Steele tells us that more than nine thousand copies of each volume were sold off.[2]

Nothing could have been better timed than the appearance of the *Spectator*; it may indeed be doubted whether it could have been produced with success at any other period. Had it been projected earlier, while

[1] *Spectator*, No. 10. [2] *Ibid.*, No. 555.

I

Addison was still in office, his thoughts would have been diverted to other subjects, and he would have been unlikely to survey the world with quite impartial eyes; had the publication been delayed it would have come before the public when the balance of all minds was disturbed by the dangers of the political situation. The difficulty of preserving neutrality under such circumstances was soon shown by the fate of the *Guardian.* Shortly after the *Spectator* was discontinued this new paper was designed by the fertile invention of Steele, with every intention of keeping it, like its predecessor, free from the entanglements of party. But it had not proceeded beyond the forty-first number when the vehement partizanship of Steele was excited by the Tory *Examiner;* in the 128th number appeared a letter, signed "An English Tory," calling for the demolition of Dunkirk, while soon afterwards, finding that his political feelings were hampered by the design on which the *Guardian* was conducted, he dropped it and replaced it with a paper called the *Englishman.* Addison himself, who had been a frequent contributor to the *Guardian,* did not aid in the *Englishman,* of the violent party tone of which he strongly disapproved. A few years afterwards the old friends and coadjutors in the *Tatler* and *Spectator* found themselves maintaining an angry controversy in the opposing pages of the *Old Whig* and the *Plebeian.*

CHAPTER VI.

CATO.

IT is a peculiarity in Addison's life that Fortune, as if conspiring with the happiness of his genius, constantly furnished him with favourable opportunities for the exercise of his powers. The pension granted him by Halifax enabled him, while he was yet a young man, to add to his knowledge of classical literature an intimate acquaintance with the languages and governments of the chief European states. When his fortunes were at the lowest ebb on his return from his travels his introduction to Godolphin by Halifax, the consequence of which was *The Campaign*, procured him at once celebrity and advancement. The appearance of the *Tatler*, though due entirely to the invention of Steele, prepared the way for development of the genius that prevailed in the *Spectator*. But the climax of Addison's good fortune was certainly the successful production of *Cato*, a play which, on its own merits, might have been read with interest by the scholars of the time, but which could scarcely have succeeded on the stage if it had not been appropriated and made part of our national life by the violence of political passion.

Addison had not the genius of a dramatist. The grace, the irony, the fastidious refinement which give

him such an unrivalled capacity in describing and criticising the humours of men as a *spectator* did not qualify
him for imaginative sympathy with their actions and
passions.   But, like most men of ability in that period,
his thoughts were drawn towards the stage, and even in
Dryden's lifetime he had sent him a play in manuscript
asking him to use his interest to obtain its performance.
The old poet returned it, we are told, "with many com-
mendations, but with an expression of his opinion that on
the stage it would not meet with its deserved success."
Addison nevertheless persevered in his attempts, and
during his travels he wrote four acts of the tragedy of *Cato*,
the design of which, according to Tickell, he had formed
while he was at Oxford, though he certainly borrowed
many incidents in the play from a tragedy on the same
subject which he saw performed at Venice.[1]   It is characteristic, however, of the undramatic mood in which he
executed his task that the last act was not written till
shortly before the performance of the play, many years
later.   As early as 1703 the drama was shown to Cibber
by Steele, who said that "whatever spirit Mr. Addison
had shown in his writing it, he doubted that he would
never have courage enough to let his *Cato* stand the
censure of an English audience; that it had only been
the amusement of his leisure hours in Italy, and was
never intended for the stage."   He seems to have
remained of the same opinion on the very eve of the
performance of the play.   "When Mr. Addison," says
Pope, as reported by Spence, "had finished his *Cato* he
brought it to me, desired to have my sincere opinion of
it, and left it with me for three or four days.   I gave

---

[1] See Addison's *Works* (Tickell's edition), vol. v., p. 187.

him my opinion of it sincerely, which was 'that I
thought he had better not act it, and that he would
get reputation enough by only printing it.' This I said
as thinking the lines well written, but the piece not
theatrical enough.   Sometime after Mr. Addison said
'that his own opinion was the same with mine, but
that some particular friends of his whom he could not
disoblige insisted on its being acted.' " [1]

Undoubtedly Pope was right in principle, and anybody
who reads the thirty-ninth paper in the *Spectator* may see,
not only that Addison was out of sympathy with the
traditions of the English stage, but that his whole turn
of thought disqualified him from comprehending the
motives of dramatic composition.   "The modern drama,"
says he, " excels that of Greece and Rome in the intricacy
and disposition of the fable ; but, what a Christian writer
would be ashamed to own, falls infinitely short of it in
the moral part of the performance."   And the entire
drift of the criticism that follows relates to the thought,
the sentiment, and the expression of the modern drama,
rather than to the really essential question, the nature
of the action.   It is false criticism to say that the greatest
dramas of Shakespeare fail in morality as compared with
those of the Greek tragedians.   That the manner in
which the moral is conveyed is different in each case
is of course true, since the subjects of Greek tragedy
were selected from Greek mythology, and were treated
by Æschylus and Sophocles, at all events, in a religious
spirit, whereas the plays of Shakespeare are only indirectly
Christian, and produce their effect by an appeal to the
individual conscience.   None the less is it the case that

[1] Spence's *Anecdotes*, p. 196.

Macbeth, Hamlet, and *Lear* have for modern audiences a
far deeper moral meaning than the *Agamemnon* or the
Œdipus Tyrannus. The tragic motive in Greek tragedy
is the impotence of man in the face of moral law or
necessity; in Shakespeare's tragedies it is the corruption
of the will, some sin of the individual against the law of
God, which brings its own punishment. There was
nothing in this principle of which a Christian dramatist
need have been ashamed; and, as regards Shakespeare at
any rate, it is evident that Addison's criticism is unjust.

It is, however, by no means undeserved in its application to the class of plays which grew up after the
Restoration. Under that *régime* the moral spirit of the
Shakespearian drama entirely disappears. The king, whose
temper was averse to tragedy and whose taste had been
formed on French models, desired to see every play end
happily. "I am going to end a piece," writes Roger,
Earl of Orrery, to a friend, "in the French style, because
I have heard the King declare that he preferred their
manner to our own." The greatest tragedies of the
Elizabethan age were transformed to suit this new
fashion; even King Lear obtained a happy deliver-
ance from his sufferings in satisfaction of the require-
ments of an effeminate Court. Addison very wittily
ridicules this false taste in the fortieth number of the
Spectator. He is not less felicitous in his remarks on the
sentiments and the style of the Caroline drama, though he
does not sufficiently discriminate his censure, which he
bestows equally on the dramatists of the Restoration and
on Shakespeare. Two main characteristics appear in all
the productions of the former epoch—the monarchical
spirit and the fashion of gallantry. The names of the

plays speak for themselves : on the one hand, *The Indian Emperor, Aurengzebe, The Indian Queen, The Conquest of Granada, The Fate of Hannibal;* on the other, *Secret Love, Tyrannic Love, Love and Vengeance, The Rival Queens, Theodosius, or the Power of Love,* and numberless others of the same kind.   In the one set of dramas the poet sought to arouse the passion of pity by exhibiting the downfall of persons of high estate ; in the other he appealed to the sentiment of romantic passion.   Such were the fruits of that taste for French romance which was encouraged by Charles II., and which sought to disguise the absence of genuine emotion by the turgid bombast of its sentiment and the epigrammatic declamation of its rhymed verse.

At the same time the taste of the nation having been once turned into French channels, a remedy for these defects was naturally sought for from French sources ; and just as the school of Racine and Boileau set its face against the extravagances of the romantic coteries, so Addison and his English followers, adopting the principles of the French classicists, applied them to the reformation of the English theatre.   Hence arose a great revival of respect for the poetical doctrines of Aristotle, regard for the unities of time and place, attention to the proprieties of sentiment and diction—in a word, for all those characteristics of style afterwards summed up in the phrase " correctness."

This habit of thought, useful as an antidote to extravagance, was not fertile as a motive of dramatic production.   Addison worked with strict and conscious attention to his critical principles : the consequence is that his *Cato,* though superficially " correct," is a passionless and mechanical play.   He had combated with reason the

"ridiculous doctrine in modern criticism, that writers of
tragedy are obliged to an equal distribution of rewards
and punishments, and an impartial execution of poetical
justice."[1]   But his reasoning led him on to deny that the
idea of justice is an essential element in tragedy.   "We
find," says he, "that good and evil happen alike to all
men on this side the grave; and, as the principle design
of tragedy is to raise commiseration and terror in the
minds of the audience, we shall defeat this great end if
we always make virtue and innocence happy and successful. . . . The ancient writers of tragedy treated men in
their plays as they are dealt with in the world, by making
virtue sometimes happy and sometimes miserable, as they
found it in the fable which they made choice of, or as it
might affect their audience in the most agreeable manner."[2]   But it is certain that the fable which the two
greatest of the Greek tragedians "made choice of" was
always of a religious nature, and that the idea of Justice
was never absent from it; it is also certain that Retribu-
tion is a vital element in all the tragedies of Shakespeare.
The notion that the essence of tragedy consists in the spectacle of a good man struggling with adversity is a conception derived through the French from the Roman Stoics;
it is not found in the works of the greatest tragic poets.

This, however, was Addison's central motive, and this
is what Pope, in his famous Prologue, assigns to him as
his chief praise.

> " Our author shuns by vulgar springs to move
> The hero's glory or the virgin's love ;
> In pitying love we but our weakness show,
> And wild ambition well deserves its woe.

---

[1] *Spectator*, No. 40.   [2] *Ibid.*

Here tears shall flow from a more generous cause,
Such tears as patriots shed for dying laws :
He bids your breasts with ancient ardour rise
And calls forth Roman drops from British eyes.
Virtue confessed in human shape he draws,
What Plato thought, and godlike Cato was :
No common object to your sight displays,
But what with pleasure heav'n itself surveys ;
A brave man struggling in the storms of fate,
And greatly falling with a falling state."

A falling state offers a tragic spectacle to the thought
and the reason, but not one that can be represented on
the stage so as to move the passions of the spectators.
The character of Cato, as exhibited by Addison, is an
abstraction, round which a number of other lay figures
are skilfully grouped for the delivery of lofty and appropriate sentiments.   Juba, the virtuous young prince of
Numidia, the admirer of Cato's virtue, Portius and
Marcus, Cato's virtuous sons, and Marcia, his virtuous
daughter, are all equally admirable and equally lifeless.
Johnson's criticism of the play leaves little to be said.

"About things," he observes, " on which the public
thinks long it commonly attains to think right ; and of *Cato*
it has not been unjustly determined that it is rather a poem
in dialogue than a drama, rather a succession of just sentiments in elegant language than a representation of natural
affections, or of any state probable or possible in human life.
Nothing here 'excites or assuages emotion ;' here is 'no
magical power of raising fantastic terror or wild anxiety.'
The events are expected without solicitude, and are remembered without joy or sorrow. Of the agents we have no care ;
we consider not what they are doing or what they are suffering ; we wish only to know what they have to say. Cato is
a being above our solicitude ; a man of whom the gods take
care, and whom we leave to their care with heedless confidence.   To the rest neither gods nor men can have much

attention, for there is not one among them that strongly
attracts either affection or esteem. But they are made the
vehicles of such sentiments and such expressions that there is
scarcely a scene in the play which the reader does not wish
to impress upon his memory."

To this it may be added that, from the essentially
undramatic bent of Addison's genius, whenever he con-
trives a train of incident he manages to make it a little
absurd. Dennis has pointed out with considerable humour
the consequences of his conscientious adherence to the
unity of place, whereby every species of action in the play,
love-making, conspiracy, debating, and fighting, is made
to take place in the 'large hall in the governor's palace
of Utica.'   It is strange that Addison's keen sense of the
ridiculous, which inspired so happily his criticisms on the
allegorical paintings at Versailles,[1] should not have shown
him the incongruities which Dennis discerned ; but, in
truth, they pervade the atmosphere of the whole play.
All the actors—the distracted lovers, the good young
man, Juba, and the blundering conspirator, Sempronius—
seem to be oppressed with an uneasy consciousness that
they have a character to sustain and are not confident of
coming up to what is expected of them. This is especially
the case with Portius, a pragmatic young Roman, whose
praiseworthy but futile attempts to unite the qualities of
Stoical fortitude, romantic passion, and fraternal loyalty,
exhibit him in a position of almost comic embarrassment.
According to Pope, "the love part was flung in after,
to comply with the popular taste ;" but the removal of
these scenes would make the play so remarkably barren
of incident that it is a little difficult to credit the statement.

[1] See p. 45.

The deficiencies of *Cato* as an acting play were, however, more than counterbalanced by the violence of party spirit, which insisted on investing the comparatively tame sentiments assigned to the Roman champions of liberty with a pointed modern application.   In 1713 the rage of the contending factions was at its highest point.   The Tories were suspected, not without reason, of designs against the Act of Settlement; the Whigs, on the other hand, were still suffering in public opinion from the charge of having for their own advantage protracted the war with Louis XIV.   Marlborough had been accused in 1711 of receiving bribes while commander-in-chief, and had been dismissed from all his employments.   Disappointment, envy, revenge, and no doubt a genuine apprehension for the public safety, inspired the attacks of the Whigs upon their rivals; and when it was known that Addison had in his drawers an unfinished play on so promising a subject as *Cato*, great pressure was put upon him by his friends to complete it for the stage. Somewhat unwillingly, apparently, he roused himself to the task.   So small, indeed, was his inclination for it, that he is said in the first instance to have asked Hughes, afterwards author of the *Siege of Damascus*, to write a fifth act for him.   Hughes undertook to do so, but on returning a few days afterwards with his own performance, he found that Addison had himself finished the play.   In spite of the judgment of the critics, *Cato* was quickly hurried off for rehearsal, doubtless with many fears on the part of the author.   His anxieties during this period must have been great.   "I was this morning," writes Swift to Stella on the 6th of April, "at ten at the rehearsal of Mr. Addison's play, called *Cato*, which is to

be acted on Friday. There was not half a score of us to
see it. We stood on the stage, and it was foolish enough
to see the actors prompted every moment, and the poet
directing them, and the drab that acts Cato's daughter
(Mrs. Oldfield) out in the midst of a passionate part, and
then calling out ' What's next ?' "

Mrs. Oldfield not only occasionally forgot the poet's
text; she also criticised it. She seems to have objected
to the original draft of a speech of Portius in the second
scene of the third act; and Pope, whose advice Addison
appears to have frequently asked, suggested the present
reading :

> " Fixt in astonishment, I gaze upon thee
> Like one just blasted by a stroke from heaven
> Who pants for breath, and *stiffens, yet alive,*
> In dreadful looks : a monument of wrath." [1]

Pope also proposed the alteration of the last line in the
play from

> " And oh, 'twas this that ended Cato's life,"

to

> " And robs the guilty world of Cato's life ; "

and he was generally the cause of many modifications.
"I believe," said he to Spence, " Mr. Addison did not
leave a word unchanged that I objected to in his *Cato*." [2]

On the 13th of April the play was ready for performance, and contemporary accounts give a vivid picture of
the eagerness of the public, the excitement of parties,
and the apprehensions of the author. " On our first
night of acting it," says Cibber in his Apology, speaking
of the subsequent representation at Oxford, " our house
was, in a manner, invested, and entrance demanded by

[1] Spence's *Anecdotes*, p. 151.   [2] *Ibid.*, p. 151.

twelve o'clock at noon; and before one it was not wide
enough for many who came too late for their places.   The
same crowds continued for three days together—an uncommon curiosity in that place; and the death of Cato
triumphed over the injuries of Cæsar everywhere."   The
prologue — a very fine one—was contributed by Pope;
the epilogue—written, according to the execrable taste
fashionable after the Restoration, in a comic vein—by
Garth.   As to the performance itself, a very lively record
of the effect it produced remains in Pope's letter to
Trumbull of the 30th April 1713 :—

> " Cato was not so much the wonder of Rome in his days,
> as he is of Britain in ours; and though all the foolish industry
> possible had been used to make it thought a party play, yet
> what the author said of another may the most properly be
> applied to him on this occasion :
>
>> ' Envy itself is dumb, in wonder lost,
>> And factions strive who shall applaud him most !' [1]

The numerous and violent claps of the Whig party on the one
side of the theatre were echoed back by the Tories on the
other; while the author sweated behind the scenes with concern to find their applause proceeding more from the hand
than the head.   This was the case, too, with the Prologue-
writer, who was clapped into a staunch Whig at the end of
every two lines.   I believe you have heard that, after all the
applauses of the opposite faction, my Lord Bolingbroke sent
for Booth, who played Cato, into the box, between one of the
acts, and presented him with fifty guineas, in acknowledgment,
as he expressed it, for defending the cause of liberty so well
against a perpetual dictator.   The Whigs are unwilling to be
distanced this way, and therefore design a present to the same
Cato very speedily; in the meantime they are getting ready
as good a sentence as the former on their side; so betwixt

---

[1] These lines are to be found in *The Campaign*, see p. 66.

them it is probable that Cato (as Dr. Garth expressed it) may
have something to live upon after he dies."

The Queen herself partook, or feigned to partake, of
the general enthusiasm, and expressed a wish that the
play should be dedicated to her. This honour had, however, been already designed by the poet for the Duchess
of Marlborough, so that, finding himself unable under the
circumstances to fulfil his intentions, he decided to leave
the play without any dedication. *Cato* ran for the then
unprecedented period of thirty-five nights. Addison
appears to have behaved with great liberality to the actors,
and, at Oxford, to have handed over to them all the
profits of the first night's performance; while they in
return, Cibber tells us, thought themselves "obliged to
spare no pains in the proper decorations" of the piece.
The fame of *Cato* spread from England to the Continent. It was twice translated into Italian, twice
into French, and once into Latin; a French and a German imitation of it were also published. Voltaire, to
whom Shakespeare appeared no better than an inspired
barbarian, praises it in the highest terms. " *The first
English writer who composed a regular tragedy* and infused
a spirit of elegance through every part of it was," says
he, " the illustrious Mr. Addison. His *Cato* is a master-
piece, both with regard to the diction and the harmony
and beauty of the numbers. The character of Cato is,
in my opinion, greatly superior to that of Cornelia in the
Pompey of Corneille, for Cato is great without anything
of fustian, and Cornelia, who besides is not a necessary
character, tends sometimes to bombast." Even he, however, could not put up with the love-scenes.

> " Addison l'a déjà tenté ;
> C'étoit le poëte des sages,
> Mais il étoit trop concerté,
> Et dans son Caton si vanté
> Les deux filles en vérité,
> Sont d'insipides personnages.
> Imitez du grand Addison
> Seulement ce qu'il a de bon."

There were, of course, not wanting voices of detraction. A graduate of Oxford attacked *Cato* in a pamphlet entitled *Mr. Addison turned Tory*, in which the party spirit of the play was censured. Dr. Sewell, a well-known physician of the day—afterwards satirised by Pope as " Sanguine Sewell "—undertook Addison's defence, and showed that he owed his success to the poetical, and not to the political merits of his drama. A much more formidable critic appeared in John Dennis, a specimen of whose criticism on *Cato* is preserved in Johnson's *Life*, and who, it must be owned, went a great deal nearer the mark in his judgment than did Voltaire. Dennis had many of the qualities of a good critic. Though his judgment was often overborne by his passion, he generally contrived to fasten on the weak points of the works which he criticised, and he at once detected the undramatic character of *Cato*. His ridicule of the absurdities arising out of Addison's rigid observance of the unity of place is extremely humorous and quite unanswerable. But, as usual, he spoiled his case by the violence and want of discrimination in his censure, which betrayed too plainly the personal feelings of the writer. It is said that Dennis was offended with Addison for not having adequately exhibited his talents in the *Spectator* when mention was made of his works, and he certainly did complain in a published

letter that Addison had chosen to quote a couplet from
his translation of Boileau in preference to another from a
poem on the battle of Ramilies, which he himself thought
better of.   But the fact seems to have been overlooked
that Dennis had other grounds for resentment.   In the
40th number of the *Spectator* the writer speaks of "a
ridiculous doctrine of modern criticism, that they (tragic
writers) are obliged to an equal distribution of rewards
and punishments, and an impartial execution of poetical
justice."   This was a plain stroke at Dennis, who was a
well-known advocate of the doctrine ; and a considerable
portion of the critic's gall was therefore expended on
Addison's violation of the supposed rule in *Cato.*

Looking at *Cato* from Voltaire's point of view—which
was Addison's own—and having regard to the spirit of
elegance infused through every part of it, there is much
to admire in the play.   It is full of pointed sentences,
such as—

> " 'Tis not in mortals to command success,
>   But we'll do more, Sempronius, we'll deserve it."

It has also many fine descriptive passages, the best of
which, perhaps, occurs in the dialogue between Syphax
and Juba respecting civilised and barbarian virtues :

> " Believe me, prince, there's not an African
>   That traverses our vast Numidian deserts
>   In quest of prey, and lives upon his bow,
>   But better practises these boasted virtues.
>   Coarse are his meals, the fortune of the chase,
>   Amidst the running streams he slakes his thirst,
>   Toils all the day, and at th' approach of night
>   On the first friendly bank he throws him down,
>   Or rests his head upon a rock till morn :

> Then rises fresh, pursues his wonted game,
> And if the following day he chance to find
> A new repast, or an untasted spring,
> Blesses his stars, and thinks it luxury."

But in all those parts of the poem where action and not
ornament is demanded, we seem to perceive the work of
a poet who was constantly thinking of what his characters
ought to say in the situation, rather than of one who was
actually living with them in the situation itself.   Take
Sempronius' speech to Syphax describing the horrors of
the conspirator's position:

> " Remember, Syphax, we must work in haste :
> O think what anxious moments pass between
> The birth of plots and their last fatal period.
> Oh ! 'tis a dreadful interval of time,
> Filled up with horror all, and big with death !
> Destruction hangs on every word we speak,
> On every thought, till the concluding stroke
> Determines all, and closes our design."

Compare with this the language of real tragedy, the
soliloquy of Brutus in *Julius Cæsar*, on which Addison
apparently meant to improve :

> " Since Cassius first did whet me against Cæsar
> I have not slept.
> Between the acting of a dreadful thing
> And the first motion, all the interim is
> Like a phantasma, or a hideous dream :
> The genius and the mortal instruments
> Are then in council ; and the state of man,
> Like to a little kingdom, suffers then
> The nature of an insurrection."

These two passages are good examples of the French
and English ideals of dramatic diction, though the lines
from *Cato* are more figurative than is usual in that play.

K

Addison deliberately aimed at this French manner. " I must observe," says he, "that when our thoughts are great and just they are often obscured by the sounding phrases, hard metaphors, and forced expressions in which they are clothed. Shakespeare is often very faulty in this particular."[1] Certainly he is; but who does not see that, in spite of his metaphoric style, the speech of Brutus just quoted is far simpler and more natural than the elegant " correctness " of Sempronius.

[1] *Spectator*, No. 39.

CHAPTER VII.

IT has been said that with *Cato* the good fortune of
Addison reached its climax. After his triumph in the
theatre, though he filled great offices in the State and
wedded " a noble wife," his political success was marred
by disagreements with one of his oldest friends ; while
with the Countess of Warwick, if we are to believe Pope,
he "married discord." Added to which he was unlucky
enough to incur the enmity of the most poignant and
vindictive of satiric poets, and a certain shadow has been
for ever thrown over his character by the famous verses
on "Atticus." It will be convenient in this chapter to
investigate, as far as is possible, the truth as to the quarrel
between Pope and Addison. The latter has hitherto
been at a certain disadvantage with the public, since
the facts of the case were entirely furnished by Pope,
and, though his account was dissected with great acute-
ness by Blackstone in the *Biographia Britannica*, the
partizans of the poet were still able to plead that his uncontradicted statements could not be disposed of by mere
considerations of probability.

Pope's account of his final rupture with Addison is
reported by Spence as follows :—" Philips seems to have

been encouraged to abuse me in coffee-houses and con-
versations : Gildon wrote a thing about Wycherley in
which he had abused both me and my relations very
grossly.   Lord Warwick himself told me one day 'that
it was in vain for me to endeavour to be well with Mr.
Addison; that his jealous temper would never admit of
a settled friendship between us; and, to convince me of
what he had said, assured me that Addison had encouraged
Gildon to publish those scandals, and had given him ten
guineas after they were published.'   The next day, while
I was heated with what I had heard, I wrote a letter to
Mr. Addison to let him know 'that I was not un-
acquainted with this behaviour of his; that, if I was to
speak severely of him in return for it, it should not be
in such a dirty way ; that I would rather tell him himself
fairly of his faults and allow his good qualities; and that
it should be something in the following manner.'   I then
subjoined the first sketch of what has since been called my
satire on Addison.   He used me very civilly ever after;
and never did me any injustice, that I know of, from that
time to his death, which was about three years after." [1]

Such was the story told by Pope in his own defence
against the charge that he had written and circulated the
lines on Addison after the latter's death.   In confirmation of his evidence, and in proof of his own good feeling
for, and open dealing with Addison, he inserted in the
so-called authorised edition of his correspondence in 1737
several letters written apparently to Addison, while in
what he pretended to be the surreptitious edition of 1735
appeared a letter to Craggs, written in July 1715, which,
as it contained many of the phrases and expressions used

[1] Spence's *Anecdotes*, pp. 148-149.

in the character of Atticus, created an impression in the mind of the public that both letter and verses were written about the same time. No suspicion as to the genuineness of this correspondence was raised till the discovery of the Caryll letters, which first revealed the fact that most of the pretended letters to Addison had been really addressed to Caryll; that there had been, in fact, no correspondence between Pope and Addison; and that therefore, in all probability, the letter to Craggs was also a fictitious composition, inserted in the so-called surreptitious volume of 1735 to establish the credit of Pope's own story.

We must accordingly put aside as undeserving of credence the poet's ingeniously constructed charge, at any rate in the particular shape in which it is preferred, and must endeavour to form for ourselves such a judgment as is rendered probable by the acknowledged facts of the case. What is indisputable is that in 1715 a rupture took place between Addison and Pope in consequence of the injury which the translator of the *Iliad* conceived himself to have suffered from the countenance given to Tickell's rival performance; and that in 1723 we find the first mention of the satire upon Addison in a letter from Atterbury to Pope. The question is, what blame attaches to Addison for his conduct in the matter of the two translations; and what is the amount of truth in Pope's story respecting the composition of the verses on Atticus.

Pope made Addison's acquaintance in the year 1712. On the 20th of December 1711 Addison had noticed Pope's *Art of Criticism* in the 253d number of the *Spectator*, partly, no doubt, in consequence of his perception of the merits of the poem, but probably at the particular instiga-

tion of Steele, whose acquaintance with Pope may have
been due to the common friendship of both with Caryll.
The praise bestowed on the *Essay* (as it was afterwards
called) was of the finest and most liberal kind, and was
the more welcome because it was preceded by a censure
conveyed with admirable delicacy on " the strokes of ill-
nature " which the poem contained.   Pope was naturally
exceedingly pleased, and wrote to Steele a letter of thanks
under the impression that the latter was the writer of
the paper, a misapprehension which Steele at once
hastened to correct.   " The paper," says he, " was written by one with whom I will make you acquainted, which
is the best return I can make to you for your favour."

These words were doubtless used by Steele in the
warmth of his affection for Addison, but they also express the general estimation in which the latter was then
held.   He had recently established his man Button in a
coffee-house in Covent Garden, where, surrounded by his
little senate, Budgell, Tickell, Carey, and Philips, he
ruled supreme over the world of taste and letters.   Something, no doubt, of the spirit of the coterie pervaded the
select assembly.   Addison could always find a word of
condescending praise for his followers in the pages of the
Spectator; he corrected their plays and mended their
prologues ; and they on their side paid back their patron
with unbounded reverence, perhaps justifying the satirical
allusion of the poet to the " applause " so grateful to the
ear of Atticus :

> " While wits and Templars every sentence raise,
>   And wonder with a foolish face of praise."

Pope, according to his own account, was admitted to the
society and left it, as he said, because he found it sit

too far into the night for his health. It may, however, be suspected that the natures of the author of the *Dunciad* and of the creator of Sir Roger de Coverley, though touching each other at many points, were far from naturally congenial; that the essayist was well aware that the man who could write the *Essay on Criticism* had a higher capacity for poetry than either himself or any of his followers; and that the poet, on his side, conscious of great if undeveloped powers, was inclined to resent the air of patronage with which he was treated by the King of Button's.   Certain it is that the praise of Pope by Addison in number 253 of the *Spectator* is qualified (though by no means unjustly), and that he is not spoken of with the same warmth as Tickell and Ambrose Philips in number 523. "Addison," said Pope to Spence, "seemed to value himself more upon his poetry than upon his prose ; though he wrote the latter with such particular ease, fluency, and happiness."[1] This often happens ; and perhaps the uneasy consciousness that, in spite of the reputation which his *Campaign* had secured for him, he was really inferior to such men as John Philips and Tickell, made Addison touchy at the idea of the entire circle being outshone by a new candidate for poetical fame.

Whatever jealousy, however, existed between the two was carefully suppressed during the first year of their acquaintance.   Pope showed Addison the first draft of the *Rape of the Lock*, and, according to Warburton (whose account must be received with suspicion), imparted to him his design of adding the fairy machinery.   If Addison really endeavoured to dissuade the

[1] Spence's *Anecdotes*, p. 257.

poet from making this exquisite addition, the latter was
on his side anxious that *Cato*, which, as has been said,
was shown to him after its completion, should not be
presented on the stage ; and his advice, if tested by the
result, would have been quite as open as Addison's to
an unfavourable construction.   He wrote, however, for
the play the famous Prologue, which Steele inserted
with many compliments in the *Guardian*.   But not long
afterwards the effect of the compliments was spoiled
by the comparatively cold mention of Pope's *Pastorals*
in the same paper that contained a glowing panegyric
on the *Pastorals* of Ambrose Philips.   In revenge Pope
wrote his paper commending Philips' performance and
depreciating his own, the irony of which, it is said,
escaping the notice of Steele, was inserted by him in the
Guardian, much to the amusement of Addison and more
to the disgust of Philips.

The occasion on which Pope's pique against Addison
began to develop into bitter resentment is sufficiently
indicated by the date which the poet assigns to the first
letter in the concocted correspondence—viz. July 20,
1713.   This letter (which is taken, with a few slight
alterations of names, from one written to Caryll on
November 19, 1712) opens as follows :—

"I am more joyed at your return than I should be at
that of the sun, so much as I wish for him this melancholy
wet season; but it has a fate too like yours to be displeasing
to owls and obscure animals, who cannot bear his lustre.
What puts me in mind of these night-birds was John Dennis,
whom I think you are best revenged upon, as the sun was
in the fable upon those bats and beastly birds above mentioned, only by shining on.   I am so far from esteeming it
any misfortune, that I congratulate you upon having your

share in that which all the great men and all the good men
that ever lived have had their part of—envy and calumny.
To be uncensured and to be obscure is the same thing. You
may conclude from what I here say that it was never in my
thoughts to have offered you my pen in any direct reply to
such a critic, but only in some little raillery, not in defence
of you, but in contempt of him."

The allusion is to the squib called *Dr. Norris' Narrative of the Frenzy of John Dennis*, which, it appears, was
shown to Addison by Pope before its appearance, and
after the publication of which Addison caused Steele to
write to Lintot in the following terms :—

"Mr. Lintot,—Mr. Addison desired me to tell you that
he wholly disapproves the manner of treating Mr. Dennis in
a little pamphlet by way of Mr. Norris' account. When he
thinks fit to take notice of Mr. Dennis' objections to his
writings, he will do it in a way Mr. Dennis shall have no
just reason to complain of. But when the papers above
mentioned were offered to be communicated to him he said
he could not, either in honour or conscience, be privy to
such a treatment, and was sorry to hear of it.—I am, sir,
your very humble servant."

Pope's motive in writing the pamphlet was, as Johnson says, "to give his resentment full play without
appearing to revenge himself" for the attack which
Dennis had made on his own poems. Addison doubtless
divined the truth ; but the wording of the letter which
he caused a third person to write to Lintot certainly
seems studiously offensive to Pope, who had, professedly
at any rate, placed his pen at his service, and who had
connected his own name with *Cato* by the fine Prologue
he had written in its praise. Lintot would of course
have shown Pope Steele's letter, and we may be sure
that the lofty tone taken by Addison in speaking of the

pamphlet would have rankled bitterly in the poet's mind.

At the same time Philips, who was naturally enraged with Pope on account of the ridicule with which the latter had covered his *Pastorals*, endeavoured to widen the breach by spreading a report that Pope had entered into a conspiracy to write against the Whigs and to undermine the reputation of Addison. Addison seems to have lent a ready ear to these accusations. At any rate Pope thought so; for when the good-natured painter Jervas sought to bring about a composition, he wrote to him (27th August 1714):

"What you mentioned of the friendly office you endeavoured to do betwixt Mr. Addison and me deserves acknowledgment on my part. You thoroughly know my regard to his character, and my propensity to testify it by all ways in my power. You as thoroughly know the scandalous meanness of that proceeding, which was used by Philips, to make a man I so highly value suspect my disposition towards him. But as, after all, Mr. Addison must be the judge in what regards himself, and has seemed to be no very just one to me, so I must own to you I expect nothing but civility from him, how much soever I wish for his friendship. As for any offices of real kindness or service which it is in his power to do me, I should be ashamed to receive them from any man who had no better opinion of my morals than to think me a party man, nor of my temper than to believe me capable of maligning or envying another's reputation as a poet. So I leave it to time to convince him as to both, to show him the shallow depths of those half-witted creatures who misinformed him, and to prove that I am incapable of endeavouring to lessen a person whom I would be proud to imitate and therefore ashamed to flatter. In a word, Mr. Addison is sure of my respect at all times, and of my real friendship whenever he shall think fit to know me for what I am."

It is evident from the tone of this letter that all the materials for a violent quarrel were in existence. On the one side was Addison with probably an instinctive dislike of Pope's character, intensified by the injurious reports circulated against Pope in the "little senate" at Button's; with a nature somewhat cold and reserved; and with something of literary jealousy partly arising from a sense of what was due to his acknowledged supremacy, and partly from a perception that there had appeared a very formidable "brother near the throne." On the side of Pope there was an eager sensitiveness, ever craving for recognition and praise, with an abnormal irritability prone to watch for, and reluctant to forgive, anything in the shape of a slight or an injury. Slights and injuries he already deemed himself to have received, and accordingly, when Tickell in 1715 published his translation of the first book of the *Iliad* at the same time with his own translation of the first four books, his smothered resentment broke into a blaze at what he imagined to be a conspiracy to damage his poetical reputation. Many years afterwards, when the quarrel between Addison and himself had become notorious, he arranged his version of it for the public in a manner which is indeed far from assisting us to a knowledge of the truth, but which enables us to understand very clearly what was passing in his own mind at the time.

The subscription for Pope's translation of the *Iliad* was set on foot in November 1713. On the 10th October 1714, having two books completed, he wished to submit them—or at any rate he told the public so in 1735—to Addison's judgment. This was at a date when, as he informed Spence, "there had been a coldness between

Mr. Addison and me " for some time.   According to the
letter which appears in his published correspondence, he
wrote to Addison on the subject as follows :—

"I have been acquainted by one of my friends, who
omits no opportunities of gratifying me, that you have lately
been pleased to speak of me in a manner which nothing but
the real respect I have for you can deserve.   May I hope
that some late malevolences have lost their effect ? . . .
As to what you have said of me I shall never believe that
the author of *Cato* can speak one thing and think another.
As a proof that I account you sincere, I beg a favour of you,
—it is that you would look over the two first books of my
translation of Homer, which are in the hands of Lord Halifax.   I am sensible how much the reputation of any poetical
work will depend upon the character you give it.   It is
therefore some evidence of the trust I repose in your good
will when I give you this opportunity of speaking ill of me
with justice, and yet expect you will tell me your truest
thoughts at the same time you tell others your most favourable ones." [1]

Whether the facts reported in this letter were as
fictitious as we have a right to assume the letter itself
to be, it is impossible to say ; Pope at any rate told
Spence the following story, which is clearly meant to
fall in with the evidence of the correspondence :—

" On his meeting me there " (Button's Coffee House) " he
took me aside and said he should be glad to dine with me at
such a tavern if I would stay till those people (Budgell and
Philips) were gone.   We went accordingly, and after dinner
Mr. Addison said ' that he had wanted for some time to
talk with me : that his friend Tickell had formerly, while at
Oxford, translated the first book of the *Iliad*.   That he now
designed to print it ; and had desired him to look it over :
he must therefore beg that I would not desire him to look
over my first book, because, if he did, it would have the air

---

[1] Pope's *Works*, Elwin and Courthope's edition, vol. vi. p. 408.

of double dealing.' I assured him that I did not take it ill
of Mr. Tickell that he was going to publish his translation;
that he certainly had as much right to translate any author
as myself; and that publishing both was entering on a fair
stage. I then added 'that I would not desire him to look
over my first book of the *Iliad* because he had looked over
Mr. Tickell's; but could wish to have the benefit of his
observations on my second, which I had then finished, and
which Mr. Tickell had not touched upon.' Accordingly I
sent him the second book the next morning; and in a few
days he returned it with very high commendation. Soon
after it was generally known that Mr. Tickell was publishing
the first book of the *Iliad* I met Dr. Young in the street,
and upon our falling into that subject, the doctor expressed
a great deal of surprise at Tickell's having such a translation
by him so long. He said that it was inconceivable to him;
and that there must be some mistake in the matter: that he
and Tickell were so intimately acquainted at Oxford that
each used to communicate to the other whatever verses they
wrote, even to the least things: that Tickell could not have
been busied in so long a work there without his knowing
something of the matter; and that he had never heard a
single word of it till this occasion."[1]

It is scarcely necessary to say that, after the light
that has been thrown on Pope's character by the de-
tection of the frauds he practised in the publication of
his correspondence, it is impossible to give any credence
to the tales he poured into Spence's ear tending to
blacken Addison's character and to exalt his own.
Tickell's MS. of the translation is in existence, and all
the evidence tends to show that he was really the
author of it. But the above statement may be taken to
reflect accurately enough the rage, the resentment, and
the suspicion which disturbed Pope's own mind on the
appearance of the rival translation. We can scarcely

[1] Spence's *Anecdotes*, p. 146.

doubt that it was this, and this alone, which roused him
to such glowing indignation, and inspired him to write
the character of Atticus. When the verses were made
public, after Addison's death, he probably perceived
that the public would not consider the evidence for
Addison's collusion with Tickell to be sufficiently strong
to afford a justification for the bitterness of the satire.
It was necessary to advance some stronger plea for such
retaliation, especially as rumour confidently asserted
that the lines had not been written till after Addison
was dead. Hence the story told by Pope to Spence,
proving first that the lines were not only written
during Addison's lifetime, but were actually sent to
Addison himself; and secondly, that they were only
composed after the strongest evidence had been afforded
to the poet of his rival's malignant disposition towards
him. Hence, too, the publication in 1735 of the letter
to Craggs, which, containing as it did many of the
phrases and metaphors employed in the verses, seemed
to supply indirect evidence that both were written
about the same period.

With regard to Pope's story it is not too much to
say that it entirely breaks down on examination. He
professes to give it on the authority of Lord Warwick
himself, reckoning, of course, that the evidence of Addison's own stepson would be conclusive with the public.
But Addison was not married to the Countess of Warwick till August 1716 ; and in the previous May he
had bestowed the most liberal praise on Pope's translation in one of his papers in the *Freeholder*. For Lord
Warwick therefore to argue at that date that Addison's
"*jealous temper* could never admit of a settled friend-

ship" between him and Pope was out of the question.
If, on the other hand, Lord Warwick told his story to
Pope before his mother's marriage, the difficulty is
equally great.   The letter to Craggs, which, if it was
ever sent to the latter at all, must obviously have
been written in the same "heat" which prompted the
satire on Atticus, is dated July 15, 1715. This fits in
well enough with the date of the dispute about the rival
translations of the *Iliad*, but not with Lord Warwick's
story, for Wycherley, after whose death Gildon, we are
told, was hired by Addison to abuse Pope, did not die
till the December of that year.

Again, the internal evidence of the character itself
points to the fact that, when it was first composed, its
"heat" was not caused by any information the poet
had received of a transaction between Addison and
Gildon.   The following is the first published version of
the satire :—

> "If Dennis writes and rails in furious pet
> I'll answer Dennis when I am in debt.
> If meagre Gildon draw his meaner quill,
> I wish the man a dinner and sit still.
> But should there *One* whose better stars conspire
> To form a bard, and raise a genius higher,
> Blest with each talent and each art to please,
> And born to live, converse, and write with ease ;
> Should such a one, resolved to reign alone,
> Bear, like the Turk, no brother near the throne.
> View him with jealous yet with scornful eyes,
> Hate him for arts that caused himself to rise,
> Damn with faint praise, assent with civil leer,
> And without sneering teach the rest to sneer.
> Alike reserved to blame or to commend,
> A timorous foe and a suspicious friend,

Fearing e'en fools, by flatterers besieged,
And so obliging that he ne'er obliged;
Willing to wound, and yet afraid to strike,
Just hit the fault, and hesitate dislike,
Who when two wits on rival themes contest,
Approves of both, but likes the worst the best:
Like Cato, give his little senate laws
And sits attentive to his own applause;
While wits and templars every sentence praise
And wonder with a foolish face of praise :
Who would not laugh if such a man there be ?
Who would not weep if Addison were he ? "

There is sufficient corroborative evidence to allow us
to believe that these lines were actually written, as
Pope says, during Addison's lifetime ; and if they were,
the character of the satire would naturally suggest that
its motive was Addison's supposed conduct in the matter
of the two translations of the *Iliad.*   There is nothing
in them to indicate any connection in the poet's mind
between Gildon and Addison ; on the other hand,
the allusion to the "two wits" shows the special griev-
ance that formed the basis, in his imagination, of the
whole character.   Afterwards we find that "meaner
quill" is replaced by "*venal* quill ;" and the couplet
about the rival translations is suppressed.   The infer-
ence is plain.   When Pope was charged with having
written the character after Addison's death, he found
himself obliged, in self-defence, to furnish a moral
justification for the satire ; and, after his own unfor-
tunate manner, he proceeded to build up for himself a
position on a number of systematic falsehoods.   His
story was probably so far true that the character was
really written while Addison was alive ; on the other
hand, it is not unreasonable to conclude that the entire

statement about Gildon and Lord Warwick is fabulous; and, as the assertion that the lines were sent to Addison immediately after their composition is associated with these myths, this too may fairly be dismissed as equally undeserving of belief.

As to the truth of the character of Atticus, however, it by no means follows, because Pope's account of its origin is false, that the portrait itself is altogether untrue. The partizans of Addison endeavour to prove that it is throughout malicious and unjust. But no one can fail to perceive that the character itself is a very extraordinary picture of human nature; and there is no reason to suppose that Addison was superior to the weaknesses of his kind. On the contrary, there is independent evidence to show that he was strongly influenced by that literary jealousy which makes the groundwork of the ideal character. This the piercing intelligence of Pope no doubt plainly discerned; his inflamed imagination built up on this foundation the wonderful fabric that has ever since continued to enchant the world. The reader who is acquainted with his own heart will probably not find much difficulty in determining what elements in the character are derived from the substantial truth of nature, and what are to be ascribed to the exaggerated perceptions of Genius.

CHAPTER VIII.

THE representation of *Cato* on the stage was a turning point in the political fortunes of the Whigs. In the same month the Queen announced, on the meeting of Parliament, the signature of the Treaty of Utrecht. Whatever were the merits or demerits of the policy embodied in this instrument, it offered many points of attack to a compact and vigorous Opposition. The most salient of these was perhaps the alleged sacrifice of British commercial interests through the incompetence or corruption of the negotiators, and on this question the Whigs accordingly raised vehement and reiterated debates. Addison aided his political friends with an ingenious pamphlet on the subject called *The late Trial and Conviction of Count Tariff*, containing a narrative of the lawsuit between the Count and Goodman Fact, which is written with much spirit and pleasantry. It is said that he also took the field in answer to the Address to the Queen from the magistrates of Dunkirk, wherein Her Majesty was requested to waive the execution of the article in the Treaty providing for the demolition of the harbour and fortifications of that town; but if he wrote on the subject the pamphlet has not been preserved by Tickell. His old friend Steele was meanwhile involving himself in difficulties through the heat and impetuosity of his party passions. After the painful abstinence from partizanship imposed on him by the scheme of the *Tatler* and *Spectator* he had founded the *Guardian* on similar lines, and had carried it on in a non-political spirit up to the 128th number, when his Whig feelings could restrain themselves no longer, and he inserted a letter signed by " An English Tory," demanding the immediate demolition of Dunkirk. Soon afterwards he published a pamphlet called *The Crisis* to excite the apprehensions of the nation with regard to the Protestant succession, and, dropping the *Guardian*, started the *Englishman*, a political paper of extreme Whig views. He further irritated the Tory majority in Parliament by supporting the proposal of Sir Thomas Hanmer, as Speaker of the House of Commons, in a speech violently reflecting on the rejected Bill for a Treaty of Commerce with France. A complaint was brought before the House against the *Crisis* and two numbers of the *Englishman*, and Steel was ordered to attend and answer for his conduct. After the charge had been preferred against him, he asked for time to arrange his defence; and this being granted him after a warm debate, he reappeared in his place a few days later, and made a long and able speech, which is said to have been prepared for him by Addison, acting under the instructions of the Kit-Kat Club. It did not, however, save him from being expelled from the House.

Addison himself stood aloof, as far as was possible, from the heated atmosphere of party, occupying his

time chiefly with the execution of literary designs. In
1713 he began a work on the Evidences of Christianity,
which he never finished, and in the last half of the year
1714 he completed the eighth volume of the *Spectator*.
So moderate was his political attitude that Bolingbroke
was not without hopes of bringing him over to the Tory
side; an interview, however, convinced him that it was
useless to dream of converting Addison's steady consti-
tutional principle to his own ambitious schemes.

The condition of the Tory party was indeed rapidly
becoming desperate. Its leaders were at open variance
with each other. Oxford, a veteran intriguer, was desirous of combining with the Whigs; the more daring
and brilliant Bolingbroke aimed at the restoration of the
exiled Stuarts. His influence, joined to natural family
affection, prevailed with the Queen, who was persuaded to
deprive Oxford of the Treasurer's staff. But her health
was undermined, and a furious and indecent dispute between the two Tory leaders in her own presence completely prostrated her. She was carried from the Council,
and sinking into a state of unconsciousness from which
she never recovered, died on the 1st of August 1714.

Meantime the Whigs were united and prepared. On
the meeting of the Council George I. was proclaimed
King without opposition : Lord-Justices were authorised
to administer affairs provisionally ; and Addison was
appointed their Secretary. It is said, though on no
good authority, that having, in discharge of his office,
to announce to George I. the death of the Queen, Addison was embarrassed in his choice of phrases for the
occasion, and that the duty to which the best writer
in the *Spectator* proved unequal was performed by a

common clerk. Had Addison been quite unfamiliar
with public life this story would have been more credible,
but his experience in Ireland must have made him
acquainted with the peculiarities of official English; and
some surviving specimens of his public correspondence
prove him to have been a sufficient master in the art
of saying nothing in a magnificent way.

On the arrival of the King in England, the Earl of
Sunderland was appointed to succeed the Duke of
Shrewsbury as Lord-Lieutenant of Ireland, and he
once more offered Addison the post of Chief Secretary.
In that office the latter continued till the Earl's resignation of the Lord-Lieutenancy in August 1715. It
would appear to have been less lucrative to him than
when he previously held it, and, indeed, than he himself had expected; the cause of this deficiency being,
as he states, "his Lordship's absence from that kingdom, and his not being qualified to give out military
commissions."[1]   He is said, nevertheless, to have shown
the strictest probity and honour in his official dealings,
and some of his extant correspondence (the authenticity
of which, however, is guaranteed only by the unsatis-
factory testimony of Curll) shows him to have declined,
in a very high-minded manner, a present of money,
evidently intended to secure his interest on behalf of
an applicant.   He seems to have been in London almost
as much as in Dublin during his tenure of office, and he
found time in the midst of his public business to com-
pose another play for the stage.

For there appears to be no good reason for doubting
that *The Drummer* was the work of Addison.   It is true

[1] Addison's Memorial to the King.

that it was not included by Tickell in his edition of his friend's writings; and Steele, in the letter to Congreve which he prefixed to the second edition of the play, only says that Addison sent for him when he was a patentee of Drury Lane Theatre, and told him "that a gentleman then in the room had written a play which he was sure I should like, but it was to be a secret; and he knew I would take as much pains, since he recommended it, as I would for him." But Steele could, under such circumstances, hardly have been deceived as to the real authorship of the play, and if confirmatory evidence is required, it is furnished by Theobald, who tells us that Addison informed him that he had taken the character of Vellum, the steward, from Fletcher's *Scornful Lady*. Addison was probably not anxious himself to assert his right of paternity to the play. It was acted at Drury Lane, and, the name of the author being unknown, was coldly received; a second performance of it after Addison's death, when the authorship was proclaimed, was naturally more successful; but, in fact, the piece is, like *Cato*, a standing proof of Addison's deficiency in dramatic genius. The plot is poor and trivial, nor does the dialogue, though it shows in many passages traces of its author's peculiar vein of humour, make amends by its brilliancy for the tameness of the dramatic situation.

He was soon, however, called upon to employ his pen on a task better suited to his powers. In September 1715 there was a rising in Scotland and in the North of England on behalf of the Pretender. The rebellion was put down with little difficulty; but the position of the House of Brunswick was far more precarious than on the surface it seemed to be. It could count, no doubt, on the loyalty of a House of Commons, elected when the Tories were momentarily stunned by the death of Queen Anne, on the faith of the army, and on the support of the monied interest. On the other hand, the two most important classes in the kingdom—the landed proprietors and the clergy—were generally hostile to the new *régime*, and the influence exercised by the latter was of course exceedingly great in days when the pulpit was still the chief instrument in the formation of public opinion. The weight of some powerful writer was urgently needed on the Whig side, and Addison—who in the preceding August had been obliged to vacate his office of Secretary in consequence of the resignation of the Lord-Lieutenant—was by common consent indicated as the man best qualified for the task. There were indeed hot political partizans who questioned his capacity. Steele said that "the Government had made choice of a lute when they ought to have taken a trumpet." But if by the "trumpet" he was modestly alluding to himself, it may very well be doubted if the objects of the Government would have been attained by employing the services of the author of the *Englishman*. What was wanted was not party invective, but the calm persuasiveness of reason; a pen that could *prove* to all Tory country gentlemen and thorough - going High Churchmen that the Protestant succession was indispensable to the safety of the principles which each respectively considered to be of vital importance. This was the task which lay before Addison, and which he accomplished with consummate skill in the *Freeholder*.

The name of the new paper was selected by him in

order to suggest that property was the basis of liberty;
and his main argument, which he introduces under
constantly varying forms, is that there could be no
safety for property under a line of monarchs who
claimed the dispensing power, and no security for the
liberties of the Church under kings of an alien religion.
In order to secure variety of treatment, the exact social
position of the *Freeholder* is not defined.

> "At the same time that I declare I am a freeholder I do
> not exclude myself from any other title. A freeholder may
> be either a voter or a knight of the shire, a wit or a fox-
> hunter, a scholar or a soldier, an alderman or a courtier, a
> patriot or a stock-jobber. But I choose to be distinguished
> by this denomination, as the freeholder is the basis of all
> other titles. Dignities may be grafted upon it; but this is
> the substantial stock that conveys to them their life, taste, and
> beauty, and without which they are blossoms that would fall
> away with every shake of wind." [1]

By this means he was able to impart liveliness to his
theme, which he diversifies by philosophical disquisition;
by good-natured satire on the prejudices of the country
gentlemen; by frequent papers on his favourite subject,
"the fair sex;" and by occasional glances at literature.
Though his avowed object was to prove the superiority
of the Whig over the Tory theory of the Constitution,
his "native moderation" never deserts him, and he
often lets his disgust at the stupidity of faction and his
preference for social over political writing appear in the
midst of his argument. The best papers in the series
are undoubtedy the "Memoirs of a Preston Rebel" and
the "Tory Fox-hunter," both of which are full of the
exquisite humour that distinguishes the sketches of Sir

[1] *Freeholder*, No. 1.

Roger de Coverley. The *Freeholder* was only continued for six months (December 23, 1715 to June 9, 1716), being published every Friday and Monday, and being completed in fifty-five numbers. In the last number the essayist described the nature of his work, and gave his reasons for discontinuing it.

" It would not be difficult to continue a paper of this kind if one were disposed to resume the same subjects and weary out the reader with the same thoughts in a different phrase, or to ramble through the cause of Whig and Tory without any certain aim or method in every particular discourse. Such a practice, in political writers, is like that of some preachers taken notice of by Dr. South, who, being prepared only upon two or three points of doctrine, run the same round with their audience from one end of the year to the other, and are always forced to tell them, by way of preface, ' These are particulars of so great importance that they cannot be sufficiently inculcated.' To avoid this method of tautology, I have endeavoured to make every paper a distinct essay upon some particular subject, without deviating into points foreign to the tenor of each discourse. They are indeed most of them essays upon Government, but with a view to the present situation of affairs in Great Britain, so that, if they have the good fortune to live longer than works of this nature generally do, future readers may see in them the complexion of the times in which they were written. However, as there is no employment so irksome as that of transcribing out of one's self next to that of transcribing out of others, I shall let drop the work, since there do not occur to me any material points arising from our present situation which I have not already touched upon."

It was probably in reward for his services in publishing the *Freeholder* that he was made one of the Commissioners for Trade and Colonies. Soon after his appointment to this office he married Charlotte, Countess of Warwick, daughter of Sir Thomas Myddleton, of

Chirk Castle, Denbighshire.   His attachment to the
Countess is said to have begun years before; and this
seems not unlikely, for, though the story of his having
been tutor to the young Earl is obviously groundless,
two charming letters of his to the latter are in existence
which show that as early as 1708 he took a strong
interest in the family.   These letters, which are written
entirely on the subject of birds, may of course have
been inspired merely by an affection for the boy himself;
but it is not unreasonable to suppose that the writer felt
a yet stronger interest in the mother, though her indif-
ference, or his natural diffidence, led him to disguise his
feelings; perhaps, indeed, the episode of Sir Roger de
Coverley's love passage with the cruel widow may be
founded on personal experience.   We have seen him in
1711 reporting to a friend that the loss of his place
had involved that of his mistress.   Possibly the same
hard-hearted mistress condescended to relent when she
saw her former lover once more on the road to high
State preferment.

Report says that the marriage was not a happy one.
The tradition, however, like so many others about the
same person, seems to have been derived from Pope, who,
in his *Epistle to Arbuthnot*, congratulates himself—with an
evident glance at Addison—on "not marrying discord
with a noble wife."   An innuendo of this kind, and
coming from such a quarter, ought not to be accepted
as evidence without some corroboration, and the only
corroboration which is forthcoming is a letter of Lady
Mary Wortley Montagu, who writes from Constanti-
nople in 1717 :—"I received the news of Mr. Addison's
being declared Secretary of State with the less surprise

in that I know the post was offered to him before. At
that time he declined it; and I really believe he would
have done well to decline it now. Such a post as that,
and such a wife as the Countess, do not seem to be in
prudence eligible for a man that is asthmatic, and we
may see the day when he will be glad to resign them
both." Lady Mary, however, does not hint that Addison
was *then* living unhappily with his wife; her expressions
seem to be inspired rather by her own sharp wit and a
personal dislike of the Countess than by any knowledge of discord in the household. On the other hand,
Addison speaks of his wife in a way which is scarcely
consistent with what Johnson calls "uncontradicted
report."   On March 20th, 1718, he writes to Swift :—
"Whenever you see England your company will be the
most acceptable in the world at Holland House, where
you are highly esteemed by Lady Warwick and the
young Lord."   A henpecked husband would hardly have
invited the Dean of St. Patrick's to be the witness of
his domestic discomfort. Nor do the terms of his will,
dated only a month before his death, indicate that he
regarded his wife with feelings other than those of affection and respect : "I do make and ordain my said dear
wife executrix of this my last will; and I do appoint
her to be guardian of my dear child, Charlotte Addison,
until she shall attain her age of one-and-twenty, being
well assured that she will take due care of her education,
and provide for her in case she live to be married."   On
the whole, it seems reasonable to put positive evidence
of this kind against those vague rumours of domestic
unhappiness, which, however unsubstantial, are so easily
propagated and so readily believed.

In April 1717 the dissensions between the two sections
of the Whig Cabinet, led respectively by Townshend and
Sunderland, reached a climax, and Townshend being
worsted, Sunderland became Prime Minister.   He at
once appointed his old subordinate one of the Secretaries
of State, and Addison filled the office for eleven months.
"It is universally confessed," says Johnson, "that he
was unequal to the duties of his place."   Here again the
"universal confession" dwindles on examination to
something very different.   As far as his conduct in ad-
ministration required to be defended in Parliament, his
inaptitude for the place was no doubt conspicuous.   He
had been elected member of Parliament for Lostwithiel
in 1708, and when that election was set aside he was
chosen for Malmesbury, a seat which he retained for the
rest of his life.   He made, however, but one effort to
address the House, when, being confused with the cheers
which greeted him, he was unable to complete his sentence, and, resuming his seat, never again opened his lips.

But in other respects the evidence of his official
incapacity seems to proceed solely from his enemies.
"Mr. Addison," said Pope to Spence, "could not give
out a common order in writing from his endeavouring
always to word it too finely.   He had too beautiful an
imagination to make a man of business." [1]   Copies of
official letters and despatches written by Addison are,
however, in existence, and prove him to have been a
sufficient master of a business style, so that, though
his lack of ability as a speaker may well have impaired his efficiency as a member of the Government,
Johnson has little warrant for saying that "*finding by*

[1] Spence's *Anecdotes*, p. 175.

experience his own inability, he was forced to solicit his dismission with a pension of fifteen hundred pounds a year." As a matter of fact, Addison's own petition to the King and his private correspondence prove with sufficient clearness that his resignation was caused entirely by his failing health; while the congratulatory Latin verses addressed to him by Vincent Bourne on his recovery from one of his seizures of asthma show that his illness was of the most serious nature.

He resigned his post, however, in March 1718 with cheerful alacrity, and appears to have looked forward to an active period of literary work, for we are told that he meditated a tragedy on the death of Socrates, as well as the completion of his book on the Evidences of Christianity. But this was not to be; the exigencies of the Ministry in the following year demanded the services of his pen. A Peerage Bill, introduced by Sunderland, the effect of which was to cause the sovereign to divest himself of his prerogative of creating fresh peers, had been vehemently attacked by Steele in a pamphlet called the *Plebeian,* published March 14, 1719, which Addison undertook to answer in the *Old Whig* (March 19). The *Plebeian* returned to the attack with spirit and with some acrimony in two numbers published March 29th and 30th, and the *Old Whig* made a somewhat contemptuous reply on April 2d. "Every reader," says Johnson, "surely must regret that these two illustrious friends, after so many years passed in confidence and endearment, in unity of interest, conformity of opinion, and fellowship of study, should finally part in acrimonious opposition. Such a controversy was ' Bellum plusquam *civile,*' as Lucan expresses it. Why could not faction find

other advocates ?   But among the uncertainties of the
human state, we are doomed to number the instability
of friendship."

The rupture seems the more painful when we find
Steele, in his third and last *Plebeian*, published April 6th,
taunting his opponent with his tardiness in taking the
field, at the very moment when his former friend and
schoolfellow—unknown to him of course—was dying.
Asthma, the old enemy that had driven Addison from
office, had returned; dropsy supervened, and he died, 17th
June 1719, at Holland House, at the early age of forty-
seven. We may imagine the grief, contrition, and remorse
that must have torn the affectionate heart of Steele when
he had found he had been vexing the last hours of one
whom, in spite of all their differences, he loved so well.
He had always regarded Addison with almost religious
reverence, which did not yield even to acts of severity
on his friend's part that would have estranged the feelings of men of a disposition less simple and impulsive.
Addison had once lent him £1000 to build a house at
Hampton Court, instructing his lawyer to recover the
amount when due.   On Steele's failure to repay the
money, his friend ordered the house and furniture to be
sold and the balance to be paid to Steele, writing to him
at the same time that he had taken the step to arouse
him from his lethargy.   B. Victor, the actor, a friend of
Steele, who is the authority for the story, says that Steele
accepted the reproof with "philosophical composure," and
that the incident caused no diminution in their friendship.   Political differences at last produced a coldness
between them, and in 1717 Steele writes to his wife,
"I ask no favour of Mr. Secretary Addison."   Great

must have been the revulsion of feeling in a man of his nature when he learned that death had now rendered impossible the renewal of the old associations. All the love, admiration, and enthusiasm for Addison, which his heart and memory still preserved, broke out in the letter to Congreve which he prefixed to *The Drummer*.

Of the closing scene of Addison's life we know little except on rumour. A report was current in Johnson's time, and reached the antiquary John Nichols at the close of the last century, that his life was shortened by over-drinking. But as usual the scandal, when traced to its source, seems to originate with Pope, who told Spence that he himself was once one of the circle at Button's, and left it because he found that their prolonged sittings were injuring his health. It is highly probable that Addison's phlegmatic temperament required to be aroused by wine into conversational activity, and that he was able to drink more than most of his companions without being affected by it; but to suppose that he indulged a sensual appetite to excess is contrary alike to all that we know of his character and to the direct evidence of Bishop Berkeley, who, writing of the first performance of *Cato*, says :—"I was present with Mr. Addison and a few more friends in a side box, where we had a table and two or three flasks of Burgundy and champagne, with which the author (who is a very sober man) thought it necessary to support his spirits."

Another story, told on the same questionable authority, represents him as having sent on his death-bed for Gay, and asked his forgiveness for some injury which he said he had done him, but which he did not specify. From the more trustworthy report of Young, we learn that he asked to see the Earl of Warwick, and said to him, "See in what peace a Christian can die;" words which are supposed to explain the allusion of the lines in Tickell's elegy—

> "He taught us how to live and (oh! too high
> The price of knowledge) taught us how to die."

His body, after lying in state in the Jerusalem Chamber, was buried by night in Westminster Abbey. The service was performed by Atterbury, and the scene is described by Tickell in a fine passage, probably inspired by a still finer one written by his own rival and his friend's satirist.

> " Can I forget the dismal night that gave
> My soul's best part for ever to the grave?
> How silent did his old companions tread,
> By midnight lamps, the mansions of the dead,
> Through breathing statues, then unheeded things,
> Through rows of warriors, and through walks of kings!
> What awe did the slow solemn march inspire,
> The pealing organ, and the pausing choir;
> The duties by the lawn-robed prelate paid,
> And the last words that dust to dust conveyed!
> While speechless o'er the closing grave we bend,
> Accept these tears, thou dear departed friend!
> Oh gone for ever; take this last adieu,
> And sleep in peace next thy loved Montague." [1]

He left by the Countess of Warwick one daughter, who lived in his old house at Bilton, and died unmarried in 1797.

[1] Tickell's *Elegy*—Compare Pope's *Eloisa to Abelard*, v. 107.

CHAPTER IX.

THE GENIUS OF ADDISON.

SUCH is Addison's history, which, scanty as it is, goes far towards justifying the glowing panegyric bestowed by Macaulay on "the unsullied statesman, the accomplished scholar, the consummate painter of life and manners, the great satirist who alone knew how to use ridicule without abusing it; who, without inflicting a wound, effected a great social reform; and who reconciled wit and virtue after a long and painful separation, during which wit had been led astray by profligacy and virtue by fanaticism." It is wanting, no doubt, in romantic incident and personal interest, but the same may be said of the life of Scott; and what do we know of the personality of Homer and Shakespeare? The real life of these writers is to be found in their work; and there too, though on a different level and in a different shape, are we to look for the character of the creator of Sir Roger de Coverley. But, while it seems possible to divine the personal tastes and feelings of Shakespeare and Scott under a hundred different ideal forms of their own invention, it is not in these that the genius of Addison most characteristically embodies itself. Did his reputation rest on *Rosamond* or *Cato* or *The Campaign*, his name

would be little better known to us than any among that
crowd of mediocrities who have been immortalised in
Johnson's *Lives of the Poets*. The work of Addison consisted in building up a public opinion which, in spite of its
durable solidity, seems, like the great Gothic cathedrals,
to absorb into itself the individuality of the architect. A
vigorous effort of thought is required to perceive how
strong this individuality must have been. We have to
reflect on the ease with which, even in these days when
the foundations of all authority are called in question,
we form judgments on questions of morals, breeding, and
taste, and then to dwell in imagination on the state of
conflict in all matters religious, moral, and artistic, which
prevailed in the period between the Restoration and the
succession of the House of Hanover. To whom do we
owe the comparative harmony we enjoy ? Undoubtedly
to the authors of the *Spectator*, and first among these by
universal consent to Addison.

Addison's own disposition seems to have been of that
rare and admirable sort which Hamlet praised in Horatio :

> " Thou hast been
> As one in suffering all that suffers nothing :
> A man that Fortune's buffets and rewards
> Has ta'en with equal thanks ; and blessed are those
> Whose blood and judgment are so well commingled
> That they are not a pipe for Fortune's finger
> To sound what stop she please."

These lines fittingly describe the patient serenity and
dignified independence with which Addison worked his
way amid great hardships and difficulties to the highest
position in the State; but they have a yet more honourable application to the task he performed of reconciling

the social dissensions of his countrymen. "The blood and judgment well commingled" are visible in the standard of conduct which he held up for Englishmen in his writings, as well as in his use of the weapon of ridicule against all aberrations from good breeding and common sense. Those only will estimate him at his true worth who will give, what Johnson says is his due, "their days and nights" to the study of the *Spectator*. But from the general reader less must be expected; and as the first chapter of this volume has been devoted to a brief view of the disorder of society with which Addison had to deal, it may be fitting in the last to indicate some of the main points in which he is to be regarded as the reconciler of parties, and the founder of public opinion.

I have shown how, after the final subversion by the Civil War of the old-fashioned Catholic and Feudal standards of social life, two opposing ideals of conduct remained harshly confronting each other in the respective moral codes of the Court and the Puritans. The victorious Puritans, averse to all the pleasures of sense, and intolerant of the most harmless of natural instincts, had oppressed the nation with a religious despotism. The nation, groaning under the yoke, brought back its banished monarch, but was soon shocked to find sensual Pleasure exalted into a worship and Impiety into a creed. Though civil war had ceased, the two parties maintained a truceless conflict of opinion: the Puritan proscribing all amusement because it was patronised by the godless malignants; the courtiers holding that no gentleman could be religious or strict in his morals without becoming tainted with the cant of the Roundheads. This harsh antagonism of sentiment is humorously illustrated by the excellent Sir

Roger, who is made to moralise on the stupidity of party
violence by recalling an incident of his own boyhood :—

"The worthy knight, being but a stripling, had occasion
to inquire which was the way to St. Anne's Lane, upon which
the person whom he spoke to, instead of answering his question, called him a young Popish cur, and asked him who
made Anne a saint. The boy, being in some confusion,
inquired of the next he met which was the way to Anne's
Lane ; but was called a prick-eared cur for his pains, and
instead of being shown the way, was told that she had been
a saint before he was born, and would be one after he was
hanged. 'Upon this,' says Sir Roger, 'I did not think it
fit to repeat the former question, but going into every lane of
the neighbourhood, asked what they called the name of that
lane.' " [1]

It was Addison's aim to prove to the contending parties what a large extent of ground they might occupy in
common. He showed the courtiers in a form of light
literature which pleased their imagination, and with a
grace and charm of manner that they were well qualified
to appreciate, that true religion was not opposed to good
breeding. To this class in particular he addressed his
papers on Devotion,[2] on Prayer,[3] on Faith,[4] on Temporal
and Eternal Happiness.[5] On the other hand, he brought
his raillery to bear on the super-solemnity of the trading
and professional classes, in whom the spirit of Puritanism
was most prevalent. "About an age ago," says he, "it
was the fashion in England for every one that would be
thought religious to throw as much sanctity as possible
into his face, and, in particular, to abstain from all appearances of mirth and pleasantry, which were looked upon
as the marks of a carnal mind. The saint was of a sor-

[1] *Spectator*, No. 125.   [2] *Ibid.*, vol. iii., Nos. 201, 207.
[3] *Ibid.*, No. 391.   [4] *Ibid.*, No. 465.   [5] *Ibid.*, No. 575.

rowful countenance, and generally eaten up with spleen and melancholy." [1]

It was doubtless for the benefit of this class that he wrote his three Essays on Cheerfulness,[2] in which the gloom of the Puritan creed is corrected by arguments founded on Natural Religion.

> "The cheerfulness of heart," he observes in a charming passage, " which springs up in us from the survey of Nature's works is an admirable preparation for gratitude. The mind has gone a great way towards praise and thanksgiving that is filled with such secret gladness. A grateful reflection on the Supreme Cause who produces it, sanctifies it in the soul, and gives it its proper value. Such an habitual disposition of mind consecrates every field and wood, turns an ordinary walk into a morning or evening sacrifice, and will improve those transient gleams of joy, which naturally brighten up and refresh the soul on such occasions, into an inviolable and perpetual state of bliss and happiness."

The same qualities appear in his dramatic criticisms. The corruption of the stage was to the Puritan, or the Puritanic moralist, not so much the effect as the cause of the corruption of society. To Jeremy Collier and his imitators the theatre in all its manifestations is equally abominable; they see no difference between Shakespeare and Wycherley. Dryden, who bowed before Collier's rebuke with a penitent dignity that does him high honour, yet rallies him with humour on this point :

> "Perhaps the Parson stretched a point too far
> When with our Theatres he waged a war;
> He tells you that this very Moral Age
> Received the first infection from the Stage;

---

[1] *Spectator*, No. 494.   [2] *Ibid.*, Nos. 381, 387, 393.

> But sure a banisht Court with Lewdness fraught
> The seeds of open Vice returning brought ;
> Thus lodged (as vice by great example thrives)
> It first debauched the daughters and the wives."

Dryden was quite right. The Court after the Restoration was for the moment the sole school of manners;
and the dramatists only reflected on the stage the inverted
ideas which were accepted in society as the standard of
good breeding. All sentiments founded on reverence
for religion, or the family, or honourable industry, were
banished from the drama because they were unaccept-
able at Court. The idea of virtue in a married woman
would have seemed prodigious to Shadwell or Wycherley;
Vanbrugh had no scruples in presenting to an audience
a drunken parson in Sir John Brute; the merchant or
tradesman seemed, like Congreve's Alderman Fondle-
wife, to exist solely that their wives might be seduced
by men of fashion. Addison and his disciples saw that
these unnatural creations of the theatre were the product of
the corruption of society, and that it was men, not institutions, that needed reform. Steele, always the first to
feel a generous impulse, took the lead in raising the tone
of stage morality in a paper which, characteristically
enough, was suggested by some reflections on a passage
in one of his own plays.[1] He followed up his attack by
an admirable criticism, part of which has been already
quoted, on Etherege's *Man in the Mode*, the hero of which,
Sir Fopling Flutter, who had long been the model of
young men of wit and fashion, he shows to be "a direct
knave in his designs and a clown in his language." [2]

As usual, Addison improves the opportunity which

---

[1] *Spectator*, No. 51.   [2] *Ibid.*, No. 65.

Steele affords him, and with his grave irony exposes
the ridiculous principle of the fashionable comedy by
a simple statement of fact.

" Cuckoldom," says he, " is the basis of most of our modern
plays.   If an alderman appears upon the stage you may be
sure it is in order to be cuckolded.   An husband that is a
little grave or elderly generally meets with the same fate.
Knights and baronets, country squires, and justices of the
quorum, come up to town for no other purpose.   I have seen
poor Dogget cuckolded in all these capacities.   In short, our
English writers are as frequently severe upon this innocent
unhappy creature, commonly known by the name of a cuckold, as the ancient comic writers were upon an eating parasite
or a vain-glorious soldier.

". . . I have sometimes thought of compiling a system of
ethics out of the writings of these corrupt poets under the
title of Stage Morality.   But I have been diverted from this
thought by a project which has been executed by an ingenious gentleman of my acquaintance.   He has composed, it
seems, the history of a young fellow who has taken all his
notions of the world from the stage, and who has directed
himself in every circumstance of his life and conversation by
the maxims and examples of the fine gentleman in English
comedies.   If I can prevail upon him to give me a copy of
this new-fashioned novel, I will bestow on it a place in my
works, and question not but it may have as good an effect upon
the drama as Don Quixote had upon romance." [1]

Nothing could be more skilful than this.   Collier's
invective no doubt produced a momentary flutter among
the dramatists, who, however, soon found they had little
to fear from arguments which appealed only to that
serious portion of society which did not frequent the
theatre.   But Addison's penetrating wit, founded as it
was on truth and reason, was appreciated by the fashionable world.   Dorimant and Sir Fopling Flutter felt

[1] *Spectator*, No. 446.

ashamed of themselves. The cuckold disappeared from
the stage. In society itself marriage no longer appeared
ridiculous.

"It is my custom," says the *Spectator* in one of his late
papers, "to take frequent opportunities of inquiring from
time to time what success my speculations meet with in the
town. I am glad to find, in particular, that my discourses on
marriage have been well received. A friend of mine gives
me to understand, from Doctor's Commons, that more licenses
have been taken out there of late than usual. I am likewise
informed of several pretty fellows who have resolved to com-
mence heads of families by the first favourable opportunity.
One of them writes me word that he is ready to enter into
the bonds of matrimony provided I will give it him under
my hand (as I now do) that a man may show his face in good
company after he is married, and that he need not be ashamed
to treat a woman with kindness who puts herself into his
power for life." [1]

So, too, in politics, it was not to be expected that Addison's moderation should exercise a restraining influence
on the violence of Parliamentary parties. But in helping
to form a reasonable public opinion in the more reflective
part of the nation at large, his efforts could not have been
unavailing. He was a steady and consistent supporter of
the Whig party, and Bolingbroke found that, in spite of his
mildness, his principles were proof against all the seductions of interest. He was, in fact, a Whig in the sense
in which all the best political writers in our literature,
to whichever party they may have nominally belonged
—Bolingbroke, Swift, and Canning as much as Somers
and Burke—would have avowed themselves Whigs, as
one, that is to say, who desired above all things to main-
tain the constitution of his country. He attached him-

[1] *Spectator*, No. 525 (By Hughes).

self to the Whigs of his period because he saw in them,
as the associated defenders of the liberties of the Parliament, the best counterpoise to the still preponderant
power of the Crown. But he would have repudiated as
vigorously as Burke the democratic principles to which
Fox, under the stimulus of party spirit, committed the
Whig connection at the outbreak of the French Revolution; and for that stupid and ferocious spirit, generated
by party, which would deny to opponents even the appearance of virtue and intelligence, no man had a more
wholesome contempt. Page after page of the *Spectator*
shows that Addison perceived as clearly as Swift the
theoretical absurdity of the party system, and tolerated
it only as an evil inseparable from the imperfection of
human nature and free institutions. He regarded it as
the parent of hypocrisy and self-deception.

"Intemperate zeal, bigotry, and persecution for any party
or opinion, how praiseworthy soever they may appear to weak
men of our own principles, produce infinite calamities among
mankind and are highly criminal in their own nature ; and
yet how many persons eminent for piety suffer such monstrous
and absurd principles of action to take root in their minds
under the colour of virtues ! For my own part I must own
I never yet knew any party so just and reasonable that a man
could follow it in its height and violence and at the same
time be innocent." [1]

As to party-writing, he considered it identical with
lying.

"A man," says he, "is looked upon as bereft of common
sense that gives credit to the relations of party-writers ;
nay, his own friends shake their heads at him and consider
him in no other light than as an officious tool or a well-
meaning idiot. When it was formerly the fashion to husband

---

[1] *Spectator*, No. 399.

a lie and trump it up in some extraordinary emergency it generally did execution, and was not a little useful to the faction that made use of it; but at present every man is upon his guard : the artifice has been too often repeated to take effect." [1]

Sir Roger de Coverley "often closes his narrative with reflections on the mischief that parties do in the country."

"There cannot," says the *Spectator* himself, " a greater judgment befall a country than such a dreadful spirit of division as rends a government into two distinct people and makes them greater strangers and more averse to one another than if they were actually two different nations. The effects of such a division are pernicious to the last degree, not only with regard to those advantages which they give the common enemy, but to those private evils which they produce in the heart of almost every particular person. This influence is very fatal both to men's morals and to their understandings ; it sinks the virtue of a nation, and not only so, but destroys even common sense." [2]

Nothing in the work of Addison is more suggestive of the just and well-balanced character of his genius than his papers on Women. It has been already said that the seventeenth century exhibits the decay of the Feudal Ideal. The passionate adoration with which women were regarded in the age of chivalry degenerated after the Restoration into a habit of insipid gallantry or of brutal license. Men of fashion found no mean for their affections between a Sacharissa and a Duchess of Cleveland, while the domestic standard of the time reduced the remainder of the sex to the position of virtuous but uninteresting household drudges. Of woman as the companion and the helpmate of man, the source of all the grace and refinements of social intercourse, no trace

---

[1] *Spectator*, No. 507.   [2] *Ibid.*, No. 125.

is to be found in the literature of the Restoration except in the Eve of Milton's still unstudied poem; it is not too much to say that she was the creation of the *Spectator*.

The feminine ideal, at which the essayists of the period aimed, is very well described by Steele in a style which he imitated from Addison :—

"The other day," he writes, in the character of a fictitious female correspondent, "we were several of us at a tea-table, and, according to custom and your own advice, had the *Spectator* read among us. It was that paper wherein you are pleased to treat with great freedom that character which you call a woman's man. We gave up all the kinds you have mentioned except those who, you say, are our constant visitants. I was upon the occasion commissioned by the company to write to you and tell you 'that we shall not part with the men we have at present until the men of sense think fit to relieve them and give us their company in their stead.' You cannot imagine but we love to hear reason and good sense better than the ribaldry we are at present entertained with, but we must have company, and among us very inconsiderable is better than none at all. We are made for the cements of society, and come into the world to create relations amongst mankind, and solitude is an unnatural being to us."[1]

In contrast with the character of the writer of this letter—a type which is always recurring in the *Spectator*—modest and unaffected, but at the same time shrewd, witty, and refined, are introduced very eccentric specimens of womanhood, all tending to illustrate the derangement of the social order, the masculine woman, the learned woman, the female politician, besides those that more properly belong to the nature of the sex, the prude and the coquette. A very graceful example of Addison's peculiar humour is found in his satire on that false ambition in women which prompts them to imitate the manners of men :—

[1] *Spectator*, No. 158.

" The girls of quality," he writes, describing the customs
of the Republic of Women, "from six to twelve years old
were put to public schools, where they learned to box and
play at cudgels, with several other accomplishments of the
same nature, so that nothing was more usual than to see a
little miss returning home at night with a broken pate or two
or three teeth knocked out of her head. They were afterwards taught to ride the great horse, to shoot, dart, or sling,
and listed themselves into several companies in order to perfect themselves in military exercises. No woman was to be
married till she had killed her man. The ladies of fashion
used to play with young lions instead of lap-dogs; and when
they had made any parties of diversion, instead of entertaining
themselves at ombre and piquet, they would wrestle and
pitch the bar for a whole afternoon together. There was
never any such thing as a blush seen or a sigh heard in the
whole commonwealth." [1]

The amazon was a type of womanhood peculiarly
distasteful to Addison, whose humour delighted itself with
all the curiosities and refinements of feminine caprice—
the fan, the powder-box, and the petticoat. Nothing
can more characteristically suggest the exquisiteness of
his fancy than a comparison of Swift's verses on a *Lady's
Dressing-Room* with the following, which evidently
gave Pope a hint for one of the happiest passages in *The
Rape of the Lock:*—

" The single dress of a woman of quality is often the
product of a hundred climates. The muff and the fan come
together from the different ends of the earth. The scarf is
sent from the torrid zone, and the tippet from beneath the
Pole. The brocade petticoat rises out of the mines of Peru,
and the diamond necklace out of the bowels of Indostan." [2]

To turn to Addison's artistic genius the crowning
evidence of his powers is the design and the execution

[1] *Spectator*, No. 434.   [2] *Ibid.*, No. 69.

of the *Spectator.*   Many writers, and among them Macaulay, have credited Steele with the invention of the
Spectator as well as of the *Tatler ;* but I think that a
close examination of the opening papers in the former
will not only prove, almost to demonstration, that on
this occasion Steele was acting as the lieutenant of his
friend, but will also show the admirable artfulness of
the means by which Addison executed his intention.
The purpose of the *Spectator* is described in the tenth
number, which is by Addison :—

> "I shall endeavour," said he, "to enliven morality with
> wit, and to temper wit with morality, that my readers may,
> if possible, both ways find their account in the speculation of
> the day.   And to the end that their virtue and discretion
> may not be short, transient, intermitting starts of thought, I
> have resolved to refresh their memories from day to day till
> I have recovered them out of that desperate state of vice and
> folly into which the age has fallen."

That is to say, his design was "to hold as 'twere
the mirror up to nature," so that the conscience of
society might recognise in a dramatic form the character
of its lapses from virtue and reason.   The indispensable
instrument for the execution of this design was the
Spectator himself, the silent embodiment of right reason
and good taste, who is obviously the conception of
Addison.

> "I live in the world rather as a spectator of mankind
> than as one of the species by which means I have made my-
> self a speculative statesman, soldier, merchant, and artizan,
> without ever meddling with any practical part in life.   I am
> very well versed in the theory of a husband, or a father, and
> can discern the errors in the economy, business, and diver-
> sion of others better than those who are engaged in them;
> as standers-by discover blots which are apt to escape those

who are in the game.   I never espoused any party with
violence, and am resolved to observe an exact neutrality
between the Whigs and Tories unless I shall be forced to
declare myself by the hostilities of either side.   In short, I
have acted in all the parts of my life as a looker-on, which is
the character I intend to preserve in this paper."

In order, however, to give this somewhat inanimate
figure life and action, he is represented as the principal
member of a club, his associates consisting of various
representatives of the chief "interests" of society.   We
can scarcely doubt that the club was part of the original
and central conception of the work, and if this be so, a
new light is thrown on some of the features in the
characters of the *Spectator* which have hitherto rather
perplexed the critics.

" The *Spectator's* friends," says Macaulay, " were first
sketched by Steele.   Four of the club—the templar, the
clergyman, the soldier, and the merchant—were uninteresting
figures, fit only for a background.   But the other two—an
old country baronet and an old town rake—though not delineated with a very delicate pencil, had some good strokes.
Addison took the rude outlines into his own hands, retouched
them, coloured them, and is in truth the creator of the Sir
Roger de Coverley and the Will Honeycomb with whom we
are all familiar."

This is a very misleading account of the matter.   It
implies that the characters in the *Spectator* were mere
casual conceptions of Steele's ; that Addison knew
nothing about them till he saw Steele's rough draft ;
and that he, and he alone, is the creator of the finished
character of Sir Roger de Coverley.   But, as a matter of
fact, the character of Sir Roger is full of contradictions
and inconsistencies ; and the want of unity which it
presents is easily explained by the fact that it is the

work of four different hands. Sixteen papers on the
subject were contributed by Addison, seven by Steele,
three by Budgell, and one by Tickell. Had Sir Roger
been, as Macaulay seems to suggest, merely the stray
phantom of Steele's imagination, it is very unlikely that
so many different painters should have busied themselves
with his portrait. But he was from the first intended
to be a *type* of a country gentleman, just as much as
Don Quixote was an imaginative representation of many
Spanish gentlemen whose brains had been turned by the
reading of romances. In both cases the type of character
was so common and so truly conceived as to lend itself
easily to the treatment of writers who approached it
with various conceptions and very unequal degrees of
skill. Any critic, therefore, who regards Sir Roger de
Coverley as the abstract conception of a single mind is
certain to misconceive the character. This error lies at
the root of Johnson's description of the knight :—

" Of the characters," says he, " feigned or exhibited in the
Spectator, the favourite of Addison was Sir Roger de Coverley,
of whom he had formed a very delicate and discriminated
idea, which he would not suffer to be violated ; and therefore
when Steele had shown him innocently picking up a girl in
the Temple and taking her to a tavern, he drew upon himself so much of his friend's indignation that he was forced
to appease him by a promise of forbearing Sir Roger
for the time to come. . . . It may be doubted whether
Addison ever filled up his original delineation. He describes his knight as having his imagination somewhat
warped ; but of this perversion he has made very little use.
The irregularities in Sir Roger's conduct seem not so much
the effects of a mind deviating from the beaten track of life
by the perpetual pressure of some overwhelming idea, as of
habitual rusticity and that negligence which solitary grandeur
naturally generates. The variable weather of the mind, the

flying vapours of incipient madness, which from time to time
cloud reason without eclipsing it, it requires so much nicety
to exhibit, that Addison seems to have been deterred from
prosecuting his own design."

But Addison never had any design of the kind.
Steele indeed describes Sir Roger in the second number
of the *Spectator* as "a gentleman that is very singular in
his behaviour," but he added that "his singularities
proceed from his good sense, and are contradictions to
the manners of the world, only, as he thinks, the world
is in the wrong." Addison regarded the knight from a
different point of view. "My friend Sir Roger," he
says, "amidst all his good qualities is *something of a
humourist;* his virtues as well as imperfections are, as it
were, tinged by a certain extravagance which makes
them particularly his, and distinguishes them from those
of other men. This cast of mind, as it is generally very
innocent in itself, so it renders his conversation highly
agreeable and more delightful than the same degree of
sense and virtue would appear in their common and
ordinary colours."

The fact is, as I have already said, that it had evidently been predetermined by the designers of the
Spectator that the Club should consist of certain recognised and familiar types; the different writers in turns
worked on these types, each for his own purpose and
according to the bent of his own genius. Steele gave
the first sketch of Sir Roger in a few rough but vigorous
strokes, which were afterwards greatly refined and altered
by Addison. In Steele's hands the knight appears indeed
as a country squire, but he has also a town-house in
Soho Square, then the most fashionable part of London.

He had apparently been originally "a fine gentleman," and only acquired his old-fashioned rusticity of manners in consequence of a disappointment in love. All his oddities date from this adventure, though his heart has outlived the effects of it. "There is," we are told, "such a mirthful cast in his behaviour that he is rather beloved than esteemed." Steele's imagination had evidently been chiefly caught by the humour of Sir Roger's love affair, which is made to reflect the romantic cast of poetry affected after the Restoration, and forms the subject of two papers in the series; in two others—recording respectively the knight's kindness to his servants, and his remarks on the portraits of his ancestors—the writer takes up the idea of Addison; while another gives an account of a dispute between Sir Roger and Sir Andrew Freeport on the merits of the monied interest. Addison, on the other hand, had formed a far finer conception of the character of the country gentleman, and one that approaches the portrait of Don Quixote. As a humourist he perceived the incongruous position in modern society of one nourished in the beliefs, principles, and traditions of the old feudal world; and hence, whenever the knight is brought into contact with modern ideas, he invests his observations, as the *Spectator* says, with "a certain extravagance" which constitutes their charm. Such are the papers describing his behaviour at church, his inclination to believe in witchcraft, and his Tory principles: such, in another vein, are his criticisms in the theatre; his opinions of Spring Gardens; and his delightful reflections on the tombs in Westminster Abbey. But Addison was also fully alive to the beauty and nobility of the feudal idea, which he brings out with great

N

animation in the various papers describing the patriarchal relations existing between Sir Roger and his servants, retainers, and tenants, closing the series with the truly pathetic account of the knight's death. It is to be observed that he drops altogether Steele's idea of Sir Roger having once been a man of fashion, which is indeed discarded by Steele himself when co-operating with his friend on the picture of country life. Addison also quite disregards Steele's original hint about "the humble desires" of his hero; and he only once makes incidental mention of the widow.

Budgell contributed three papers on the subject, two in imitation of Addison; one describing a fox-hunt, and the other giving Sir Roger's opinion on beards; the third, in imitation of Steele, showing Sir Roger's state of mind on hearing of the addresses of Sir David Dundrum to the widow. The number of the *Spectator* which is said to have so greatly displeased Addison was written, not, as Johnson says, by Steele, but by Tickell. It goes far to confirm my supposition that the characters of the Club had been agreed upon beforehand. The trait which Tickell describes would have been natural enough in an ordinary country gentleman, though it was inconsistent with the fine development of Sir Roger's character in the hands of Addison.

In his capacity of critic Addison has been variously judged, and, it may be added, generally undervalued. We find that Johnson's contemporaries were reluctant to allow him the name of critic. "His criticism," Johnson explains, "is condemned as tentative or experimental rather than scientific; and he is considered as deciding by taste rather than by principles." But if Aristotle is

HIS GENIUS.

right in saying that the virtuous man is the standard of
virtue, the man of sound instincts and perceptions ought
certainly to be accepted as a standard in the more
debatable region of taste.   There can, at any rate, be
no doubt that Addison's artistic judgments founded on
instinct were frequently much nearer the mark than
Johnson's, though these were based on principle.   Again
Macaulay says : "The least valuable of Addison's con-
tributions to the *Spectator* are, in the judgment of our
age, his critical papers;" but he adds patronisingly:
"The very worst of them is creditable to him when the
character of the school in which he had been trained is
fairly considered.   The best of them were much too good
for his readers.   In truth, he was not so far behind our
generation as he was before his own."   By "the school
in which he had been trained," Macaulay doubtless
meant the critical traditions established by Boileau and
Bouhours, and he would have justified the disparage-
ment implied in his reference to them by pointing
to the pedantic intolerance and narrowness of view
which these traditions encouraged.   But in all matters
of this kind there is loss and gain.   If Addison's
generation was much more insensible than our own to a
large portion of imaginative truth, it had a far keener
perception of the laws and limits of expression; and,
granted that Voltaire was wrong in regarding Shakespeare as an "inspired barbarian," he would never have
made the mistake which critics now make every day of
mistaking nonsense for poetry

But it may well be questioned if Addison's criticism
is only "tentative and experimental."   The end of
criticism is surely to produce a habit of reasoning

rightly on matters of taste and imagination ; and, with
the exception of Sir Joshua Reynolds, no English
critic has accomplished more in this direction than
Addison. Before his time Dryden had scattered over
a number of prefaces various critical remarks admirably
felicitous in thought and racy in expression. But he
had made no attempt to write upon the subject systematically; and in practice he gave himself up without
an effort to satisfy the tastes which a corrupt Court had
formed, partly on the " false wit " of Cowley's following,
partly on the extravagance and conceit of the French
school of Romance. Addison, on the other hand, set
himself to correct this depraved fashion by establishing
in England, on a larger and more liberal basis, the standards of good breeding and common sense which Boileau
had already popularised in France. Nothing can be
more just and discriminating than his papers on the
difference between true and false wit.[1] He was the first
to endeavour to define the limits of art and taste in his
essays on the *Pleasures of the Imagination;*[2] and, though
his theory on the subject is obviously superficial, it sufficiently proves that his method of reasoning on questions
of taste was much more than " tentative and experimental." " I could wish," he says, " there were authors
who, beside the mechanical rules, which a man of very
little taste may discourse upon, would enter into the very
spirit and soul of fine writing, and show us the several
sources of that pleasure which rises in the mind on the
perusal of a noble work." His studies of the French
drama prevented him from appreciating the great Eliza-

[1] *Spectator*, Nos. 58–63, inclusive.
[2] *Ibid.*, Nos. 411–421, inclusive.

bethan school of tragedy, yet many stray remarks in
the *Spectator* show how deeply he was impressed by the
greatness of Shakespeare's genius, while his criticisms on
Tragedy did much to banish the tumid extravagance of
the romantic style. His papers on Milton achieved the
triumph of making a practically unknown poem one of
the most popular classics in the language, and he was
more than half a century before his age in his appreciation of the beauties of the English ballads. In fact,
finding English taste in hopeless confusion, he left it in
admirable order ; and to those who are inclined to
depreciate his powers as a critic the following observations of Johnson—not a very favourable judge—may be
commended :—

"It is not uncommon for those who have grown wise by
the labour of others to add a little of their own, and overlook
their masters. Addison is now despised by some who perhaps
would never have seen his defects but by the light he afforded
them. That he always wrote as he would write now cannot
be affirmed ; his instructions were such as the characters of
his readers made proper. That general knowledge, which
now circulates in common talk, was in his time rarely to be
found. Men not professing learning were not ashamed of
ignorance ; and in the female world any acquaintance with
books was distinguished only to be censured. His purpose
was to infuse literary curiosity by gentle and unsuspected
conveyance into the gay, the idle, and the wealthy : he therefore presented knowledge in the most alluring form, not lofty
and austere, but accessible and familiar. When he showed
them their defects, he showed them likewise that they might
be easily supplied. His attempt succeeded ; inquiry awakened
and comprehension expanded. An emulation of intellectual
elegance was excited, and from this time to our own life has
been gradually exalted, and conversation purified and enlarged."[1]

[1] *Life of Addison.*

The essence of Addison's humour is irony. "One slight lineament of his character," says Johnson, "Swift has preserved. It was his practice, when he found any man invincibly wrong, to flatter his opinions by acquiescence, and sink him yet deeper to absurdity." The same characteristic manifests itself in his writings under a great variety of forms. Sometimes it appears in the seemingly logical premises from which he draws an obviously absurd conclusion, as for instance :—

" If in a multitude of counsellors there is safety, we ought to think ourselves the securest nation in the world. Most of our garrets are inhabited by statesmen, who watch over the liberties of their country, and make a shift to keep themselves from starving by taking into their care the properties of all their fellow-subjects." [1]

On other occasions he ridicules some fashion of taste by a perfectly grave and simple description of its object. Perhaps the most admirable specimen of this oblique manner is his satire on the Italian opera in the number of the *Spectator* describing the various lions who had fought on the stage with Nicolini. This highly-finished paper deserves to be quoted *in extenso :*—

" There is nothing of late years has afforded matter of greater amusement to the town than Signor Nicolini's combat with a lion in the Haymarket, which has been very often exhibited to the general satisfaction of most of the nobility and gentry in the kingdom of Great Britain. Upon the first rumour of this intended combat it was confidently affirmed, and is still believed by many in both galleries, that there would be a tame lion sent from the tower every opera in order to be killed by Hydaspes. This report, though altogether groundless, so universally prevailed in the upper regions of the playhouse, that some of the refined politicians in those parts of the audience gave it out in a whisper that the lion was a cousin-

----
[1] *Spectator*, No. 556.

german of the tiger who made his appearance in King William's
days, and that the stage would be supplied with lions at the
public expense during the whole session.   Many likewise were
the conjectures of the treatment which this lion was to meet
with at the hands of Signor Nicolini; some supposed that he
was to subdue him in recitativo, as Orpheus used to serve
the wild beasts in his time, and afterwards to knock him on
the head ; some fancied that the lion would not pretend to
lay his paws upon the hero, by reason of the received opinion
that a lion will not hurt a virgin ; several, who pretended to
have seen the opera in Italy, had informed their friends that
the lion was to act a part in High Dutch, and roar twice or
thrice to a thorough-bass before he fell at the feet of Hydaspes.
To clear up a matter that was so variously reported, I have
made it my business to examine whether this pretended lion
is really the savage he appears to be or only a counterfeit.

" But before I communicate my discoveries, I must acquaint
the public that upon my walking behind the scenes last winter,
as I was thinking upon something else, I accidentally jostled
against an enormous animal that extremely startled me, and,
upon my nearer survey of it, appeared to be a lion rampant.
The lion, seeing me very much surprised, told me, in a gentle
voice, that I might come by him if I pleased ; ' for,' says he,
' I do not intend to hurt anybody.'   I thanked him very
kindly and passed by him, and in a little time after saw him
leap upon the stage and act his part with very great applause.
It has been observed by several that the lion has changed his
manner of acting twice or thrice since his first appearance ;
which will not seem strange when I acquaint my reader that
the lion has been changed upon the audience three several
times.   The first lion was a candle-snuffer, who, being a fellow
of testy choleric temper, overdid his part, and would not suffer
himself to be killed so easily as he ought to have done ;
besides it was observed of him that he became more surly
every time he came out of the lion ; and having dropped some
words in ordinary conversation as if he had not fought his
best, and that he suffered himself to be thrown on his back
in the scuffle, and that he could wrestle with Mr. Nicolini
for what he pleased out of his lion's skin, it was thought proper
to discard him, and it is verily believed to this day that, had

he been brought upon the stage another time, he would certainly have done mischief. Besides it was objected against
the first lion that he reared himself so high upon his hinder
paws and walked in so erect a posture that he looked more
like an old man than a lion.

" The second lion was a tailor by trade who belonged to
the playhouse, and had the character of a mild and peaceable
man in his profession. If the former was too furious, this
was too sheepish for his part, insomuch that after a short
modest walk upon the stage he would fall at the first touch
of Hydaspes, without grappling with him and giving him an
opportunity of showing his variety of Italian trips. It is said,
indeed, that he once gave him a rip in his flesh-coloured
doublet; but this was only to make work for himself in his
private character of a tailor. I must not omit that it was this
second lion who treated me with so much humanity behind
the scenes.

" The acting lion at present is, as I am informed, a country
gentleman, who does it for his diversion, but desires his name
may be concealed. He says, very handsomely in his own excuse,
that he does not act for gain; that he indulges an innocent
pleasure in it ; and that it is better to pass away an evening
in this manner than in gaming and drinking : but he says
at the same time, with a very agreeable raillery upon himself,
that, if his name were known, the ill-natured world might
call him ' the ass in the lion's skin.' This gentleman's temper is
made out of such a happy mixture of the mild and the choleric,
that he outdoes both his predecessors, and has drawn together
greater audiences than have been known in the memory of man.

" I must not conclude my narrative without taking notice
of a groundless report that has been raised to a gentleman's
disadvantage, of whom I must declare myself an admirer ;
namely, that Signor Nicolini and the lion have been seen
sitting peaceably by one another and smoking a pipe together
behind the scenes ; by which their common enemies would
insinuate that it is but a sham combat which they represent
upon the stage : but upon inquiry I find that if any such
correspondence has passed between them, it was not till the
combat was over, when the lion was to be looked on as dead
according to the received rules of the drama. Besides, this is

what is practised every day in Westminster Hall, where nothing is more usual than to see a couple of lawyers who have been tearing each other to pieces in the court embracing one another as soon as they are out of it." [1]

In a somewhat different vein, the ridicule cast by the *Spectator* on the fashions of his day, by anticipating the judgment of posterity on himself, is equally happy:

"As for his speculations, notwithstanding the several obsolete words and obscure phrases of the age in which he lived, we still understand enough of them to see the diversions and characters of the English nation in his time : not but that we are to make allowance for the mirth and humour of the author, who has doubtless strained many representations of things beyond the truth. For, if we must interpret his words in their literal meaning, we must suppose that women of the first quality used to pass away whole mornings at a puppet show : that they attested their principles by their patches : that an audience would sit out an evening to hear a dramatical performance written in a language which they did not understand: that chairs and flowerpots were introduced as actors upon the British stage : that a promiscuous assembly of men and women were allowed to meet at midnight in masks within the verge of the Court; with many improbabilities of the like nature. We must therefore in these and in the like cases suppose that these remote hints and allusions aimed at some certain follies which were then in vogue, and which at present we have not any notion of." [2]

His power of ridiculing keenly without malignity is of course best shown in his character of Sir Roger de Coverley, whose delightful simplicity of mind is made the medium of much good-natured satire on the manners of the Tory country-gentlemen of the period. One of the most exquisite touches is the description of the extraordinary conversion of a dissenter by the Act against Occasional Conformity.

[1] *Spectator*, No. 13.　　　[2] *Ibid.*, No. 101.

" He (Sir Roger) then launched out into praise of the late Act of Parliament for securing the Church of England, and told me with great satisfaction that he believed it already began to take effect, for that a rigid dissenter who chanced to dine in his house on Christmas day had been observed to eat very plentifully of his plum-porridge." [1]

The mixture of fashionable contempt for book-learning, blended with shrewd mother-wit, is well represented in the character of Will Honeycomb, who " had the discretion not to go out of his depth, and had often a certain way of making his real ignorance appear a seeming one." One of Will's happiest flights is on the subject of ancient looking-glasses. " Nay," says he, " I remember Mr. Dryden in his *Ovid* tells us of a swinging fellow called Polypheme, that made use of the sea for his looking-glass, and could never dress himself to advantage but in a calm."

Budgell, Steele, and Addison seem all to have worked on the character of Will Honeycomb, which, however, presents none of the inconsistencies that appear in the portrait of Sir Roger de Coverley. Addison was evidently pleased with it, and in his own inimitable ironic manner gave it its finishing touches by making Will, in his character of a fashionable gallant, write two letters scoffing at wedlock and then marry a farmer's daughter. The conclusion of the letter in which he announces his fate to the *Spectator* is an admirable specimen of Addison's humour :

" As for your fine women I need not tell thee that I know them. I have had my share in their graces, but no more of that. It shall be my business hereafter to live the life of an honest man, and to act as becomes the master of a family. I question not but I shall draw upon me the raillery of the

---

[1] *Spectator*, No. 269.

town, and be treated to the tune of "The Marriage-hater Matched;" but I am prepared for it. I have been as witty as others in my time. To tell thee truly I saw such a tribe of fashionable young fluttering coxcombs shot up that I do not think my post of an *homme de ruelle* any longer tenable. I felt a certain stiffness in my limbs which entirely destroyed the jauntiness of air I was once master of. Besides, for I must now confess my age to thee, I have been eight-and-forty above these twelve years. Since my retirement into the country will make a vacancy in the Club, I could wish that you would fill up my place with my friend Tom Dapperwit. He has an infinite deal of fire, and knows the town. For my own part, as I have said before, I shall endeavour to live hereafter suitable to a man in my station, as a prudent head of a family, a good husband, a careful father (when it shall so happen), and as

 "Your most sincere friend and humble servant,
     "WILLIAM HONEYCOMB." [1]

I have already alluded to the delight with which the fancy of Addison played round the caprices of female attire. The following—an extract from the paper on the "fair sex" which specially roused the spleen of Swift—is a good specimen of his style when in this vein :—

"To return to our female heads. The ladies have been for some time in a kind of moulting season with regard to that part of their dress, having cast great quantities of ribbon, lace, and cambric, and in some measure reduced that part of the human figure to the beautiful globular form which is natural to it. We have for a great while expected what kind of ornament would be substituted in the place of those antiquated commodes. But our female projectors were all the last summer so taken up with the improvement of their petticoats that they had not time to attend to anything else; but having at length sufficiently adorned their lower parts, they now begin to turn their thoughts upon the other ex-

---

[1] *Spectator*, No. 530.

ADDISON.

tremity, as well remembering the old kitchen proverb, 'that if you light your fire at both ends, the middle will shift for itself.' "[1]

Addison may be said to have almost created and wholly perfected English prose as an instrument for the expression of *social* thought. Prose had of course been written in many different manners before his time. Bacon, Cowley, and Temple had composed essays; Hooker, Sir Thomas Browne, Hobbes, and Locke philosophical treatises; Milton controversial pamphlets; Dryden critical prefaces; Raleigh and Clarendon histories; Taylor, Barrow, South, and Tillotson sermons. But it cannot be said that any of these had founded a prose style which, besides being a reflection of the mind of the writer, could be taken as representing the genius and character of the nation. They write as if they were thinking apart from their audience, or as if they were speaking to it either from an inferior or superior position. The essayists had taken as their model Montaigne, and their style is therefore stamped, so to speak, with the character of soliloquy; the preachers, who perhaps did more than any writers to guide the genius of the language, naturally addressed their hearers with the authority of their office; Milton, even in controversy, rises from the natural sublimity of his mind to heights of eloquence to which the ordinary idioms of society could not have borne him; while Dryden, using the language with a raciness and rhythm probably unequalled in our literature, nevertheless exhibits in his prefaces an air of deference towards the various patrons he addresses. Moreover, many of the earlier prose

[1] *Spectator*, No. 265.

writers had aimed at standards of diction which were
inconsistent with the genius of the English tongue.
Bacon, for instance, disfigures his style with the witty
antitheses which found favour with the Elizabethan and
early Stuart writers; Hooker, Milton, and Browne con-
struct their sentences on a Latin model, which, though
it often gives a certain dignity of manner, prevents anything like ease, simplicity, and lucidity of expression.
Thus Hooker delights in inversions; both he and
Milton protract their periods by the insertion of many
subordinate clauses; and Browne " projicit ampullas et
sesquipedalia verba " till the Saxon element seems almost
eliminated from his style.

Addison took features of his style from almost all his
predecessors : he assumes the characters of essayist,
moralist, philosopher, and critic, but he blends them all
together in his new capacity of journalist. He had
accepted the public as his judges; and he writes as if
some critical representative of the public were at his
elbow putting to the test of reason every sentiment and
every expression. Warton tells us in his *Essay on Pope*
that Addison was so fastidious in composition that he
would often stop the press to alter a preposition or con-
junction. And this evidence is corroborated in a very
curious and interesting manner by the MS. of some of
Addison's essays, discovered by Mr. Dykes Campbell in
1858.[1] A sentence in one of the papers on the *Pleasures
of the Imagination* shows, by the various stages through
which it passed before its form seemed satisfactory to
the writer, what nice attention he gave to the balance,

---

[1] I have to thank Mr. Campbell for his kindness and courtesy
in sending me the volume containing this collection.

rhythm, and lucidity of his periods.   In its original
shape the sentence was written thus :—

 "For this reason we find the poets always crying up a
Country Life ; where Nature is left to herself, and appears
to ye best advantage."

This is rather bald, and the MS. is accordingly corrected as follows :—

 "For this reason we find all Fancifull men, and ye poets
in particular, still in love with a Country Life ; where Nature
is left to herself, and furnishes out all ye variety of Scenes
y^t are most delightful to ye Imagination.

The text as it stands is this :—

 "For this reason we always find the poet in love with a
country life, where nature appears in the greatest perfection,
and furnishes out all those scenes that are most apt to delight
the imagination." [1]

This is certainly the best both in point of sense and
sound.   Addison perceived that there was a certain contradiction in the idea of Nature being "left to herself,"
and at the same time *furnishing* scenes for the pleasure
of the imagination : he therefore imparted the notion of
design by striking out the former phrase and substituting
' seen in perfection ; " and he emphasised the idea by
afterwards changing "delightful" into the stronger
phrase "apt to delight."   The improvement of the
rhythm of the sentence in its final form is obvious.

With so much elaboration of style it is natural that
there should be in Addison's essays a disappearance of
that egotism which is a characteristic—and a charming
one—of Montaigne ; his moralising is natural, for the
age required it, but is free from the censoriousness of

---

[1] *Spectator*, No. 414.

the preacher; his critical and philosophical papers all assume an intelligence in his reader equal to his own.

This perfection of breeding in writing is an art which vanishes with the *Tatler* and *Spectator*. Other critics, other humourists have made their mark in English literature, but no second Addison has appeared. Johnson took him for his model so far as to convey lessons of morality to the public by means of periodical essays. But he confesses that he addressed his audience in tones of " dictatorial instruction ; " and any one who compares the ponderous sententiousness and the elaborate antithesis of the *Rambler* with the light and rhythmical periods of the *Spectator* will perceive that the spirit of preaching is gaining ground on the genius of conversation. Charles Lamb, again, has passages which, for mere delicacy of humour, are equal to anything in Addison's writings. But the superiority of Addison consists in this, that he expresses the humour of the life about him, while Lamb is driven to look at its oddities from outside. He is not, like Addison, a moralist or a satirist ; the latter indeed performed his task so thoroughly that the turbulent license of Mohocks, Tityre Tus, and such like brotherhoods, gradually disappeared before the advance of a tame and orderly public opinion. To Lamb, looking back on the primitive stages of society from a safe distance, vice itself seemed pardonable because picturesque, much in the same way as travellers began to admire the loneliness and the grandeur of nature when they were relieved from apprehensions for the safety of their purses and their necks. His humour is that of a sentimentalist; it dwells on odd nooks and corners, and describes quaint survivals in men and things. For our

own age, when all that is picturesque in society is being
levelled by a dull utilitarianism, this vein of eccentric
imagination has a special charm, but the taste is likely
to be a transient one.   Mrs. Battle will amuse so long as
this generation remembers the ways of its grandmothers;
two generations hence the point of its humour will probably be lost.   But the figure of Sir Roger de Coverley,
though it belongs to a bygone stage of society, is as
durable as human nature itself, and while the language
lasts the exquisite beauty of the colours in which it is
preserved will excite the same kind of pleasure.   Scarcely
below the portrait of the good knight will be ranked the
character of his friend and biographer, the silent Spectator of men.   A grateful posterity, remembering what
it owes to him, will continue to assign him the reputation he coveted : "It was said of Socrates that he
brought philosophy down from heaven to inhabit among
men ; and I shall be ambitious to have it said of me
that I have brought philosophy out of closets and
libraries, schools and colleges, to dwell at clubs and
assemblies, at tea-tables and in coffee-houses."

THE END.

Printed by R. & R. CLARK, *Edinburgh.*

www.ingramcontent.com/pod-product-compliance
Ingram Content Group UK Ltd.
Pitfield, Milton Keynes, MK11 3LW, UK
UKHW012345130625
459647UK00009B/539